Strands

Creating Unexpected Fabrics and Fashionable Projects

Jacqueline Myers-Cho

NORTH LIGHT BOOKS

CINCINNATI, OH
www.mycraftivity.com

Other fine North Light Books are available from your local bookstore, art supply store, online supplier or visit our website at www.fwmedia.com.

13 12 11 10 09   5 4 3 2 1

Distributed in Canada by Fraser Direct
100 Armstrong Avenue
Georgetown, ON, Canada L7G 5S4
Tel: (905) 877-4411

Distributed in the U.K. and Europe by David & Charles
Brunel House, Newton Abbot, Devon, TQ12 4PU, England
Tel: (+44) 1626 323200, Fax: (+44) 1626 323319
E-mail: postmaster@davidandcharles.co.uk

Distributed in Australia by Capricorn Link
P.O. Box 704, S. Windsor, NSW 2756 Australia
Tel: (02) 4577-3555

Library of Congress Cataloging-in-Publication Data

Editors: Robin M. Hampton and Tonia Davenport
Designer: Geoff Raker and Guy Kelly
Production Coordinator: Greg Nock
Photographers: Ric Deliantoni, Christine Polomsky, Tim Grondin and Al Parrish
Stylists: Monica Skrzelowski and Nora Martini
Hair and Makeup: Lynn Molitor

Metric Conversion Chart

to convert	to	multiply by
Inches	Centimeters	2.54
Centimeters	Inches	0.4
Feet	Centimeters	30.5
Centimeters	Feet	0.03
Yards	Meters	0.9
Meters	Yards	1.1
Sq. Inches	Sq. Centimeters	6.45
Sq. Centimeters	Sq. Inches	0.16
Sq. Feet	Sq. Meters	0.09
Sq. Meters	Sq. Feet	10.8
Sq. Yards	Sq. Meters	0.8
Sq. Meters	Sq. Yards	1.2
Pounds	Kilograms	0.45
Kilograms	Pounds	2.2
Ounces	Grams	28.3
Grams	Ounces	0.035

Dedication

I dedicate this book to my beloved: my mother, father, Youngie halmuni and Youngie hal-abuji. I thank them all for holding a vision of greatness for me.

Acknowledgments

I would like to thank my loves, my husband and daughter. Their unwavering support and critiques of all my work helped to raise my book to its highest level. Thank you!

Thank you Robin, my rock and editor. This book is beautiful!

To Tonia Davenport for finding me in the sea of the web and believing in the book you saw in me.

To all of my friends, my art supporters, my teachers and to all who have crossed my path in this lifetime. I thank you all. In ways you will never know you have made me a stronger, better person and artist.

Contents

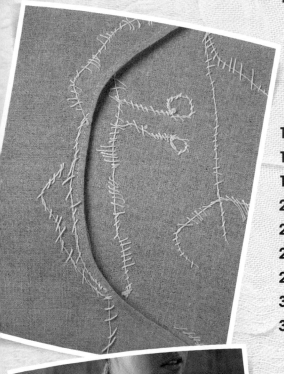

Use, Reuse, Upcycle

Have you ever been somewhere with plenty of time and a strong urge to create, but without any traditional art supplies whatsoever? In this situation, a girl must do what a girl must do.

As a child I made things from "nothing." If I didn't have any store-bought materials, I would go to my closet and cut up my least favorite article of clothing and make something new with it. It just made sense to use, reuse, upcycle and make things from scratch. So, how did the handmade fabrics featured in this book come to be? In that same line of thinking I started using the leftovers from my sewing and art projects. When I am sewing, I make a lot of waste—threads, scraps, bits of fabric everywhere. The mess is a by-product of my love of tearing fabric instead of cutting it. I learned long ago if you tear your fabric it will always be straight. When the loose threads started taking over, I began collecting them and sorting them by color.

Hence, my first thread fabric was born. The other fabrics come from my playfulness and attempts to answer the carefree question "What if?" It was through many "what-if" moments that the fabrics and projects in this book were born.

I am the kind of person who is tickled pink to eat a mixed appetizer plate rather than one type of food. I love to touch texture and even love to see texture more than color. *Strands* explores combining fine art and textiles into cool wearable projects. My goal with this book is for you to have fun! Revel in the process of making fabrics, just for the sake of making. And yes—yes, please go on out on your own tangent; let this book be your starting point! Rediscover your curious, creative inner child with wide eyes and happiness. Then wear the items you make with pride.

Tools and Supplies

Although I would encourage you to be open to using almost anything as a fabric and with your fabrics, there are certain tools that will make the work go more quickly and easily. A tool is an extension of your hand and must be comfortable, so select items that feel good to you.

Sewing Supplies

You won't see traditional sewing methods used to make the fabrics and projects in *Strands*, but you will use some conventional sewing supplies. Here are a few things you should have on hand.

Crochet thread

Wide-eye (tapestry) needle

Sewing machine

Scissors

Rotary cutter and cutting board

Ruler

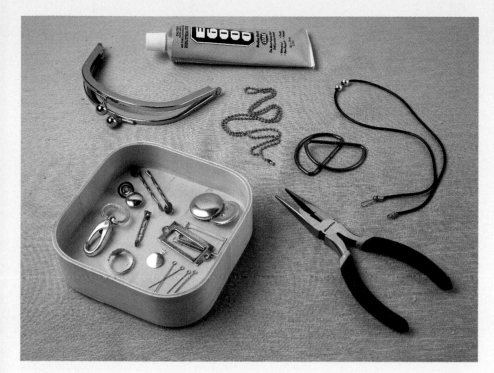

Fashion-Accessory Materials

These items will finish off your projects. Most of these items can be found at your local fabric or craft store.

- Round-nose and chain-nose pliers
- Snap-setting kit
- Ring base
- Key fob
- D rings
- Button-making kit
- Purse frame
- Pin back
- Disk bail
- Metal glue (epoxy)
- Chain
- Wire
- Bookplate

Fabric Materials

Take a good look right now in your craft room, junk drawer, garage or tool cabinet, and you'll find almost everything you need to get started making the fabrics in this book.

- Packing tape
- Plastic wrap
- Electrical tape
- White glue
- Tissue paper
- Plastic bags
- Thread
- Cardboard

Basic Sewing Stitches

As free spirits, we are here to break the rules, but you can't break a rule until you are familiar with it. I have included some basic sewing stitches and terms for your reference. The running stitch and basting stitch are done by hand, while the straight stitch, backstitch and topstitch are all done on a machine. If you are new to the sewing machine, using one is quite simple and here is your opportunity to get your feet wet.

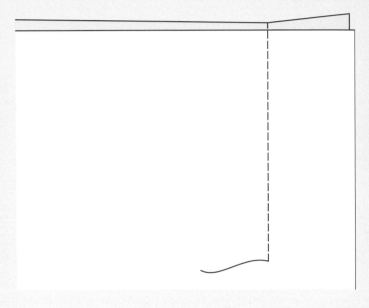

Straight Stitch

This is made with a single, forward stitch.

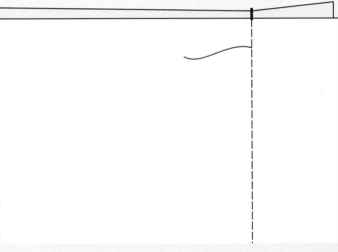

Backstitch

This means to put your machine in "reverse" by lifting (or sometimes pressing) a lever. Reversing over your stitches will lock them in and prevent your stitches from unraveling. This works with whatever type of stitch your machine is set on.

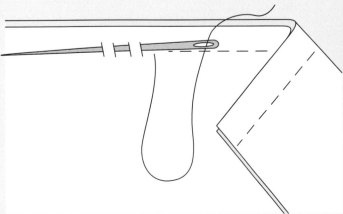

Running Stitch

This is worked by passing the needle over and under the fabric. Stiches do not overlap.

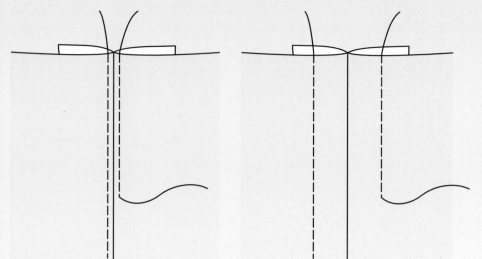

Topstitch

The topstitch is often a decorative straight stitch. Blue jeans will have a topstitch. The thread can be the same color or different than the fabric color.

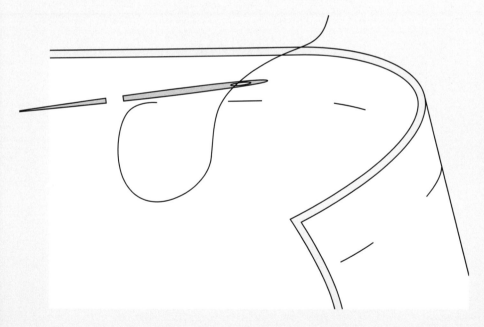

Basting Stitch

This stitch may be done by hand or machine. It is a large running stitch, used to temporarily hold together two pieces of fabric or to pull and gather the fabric.

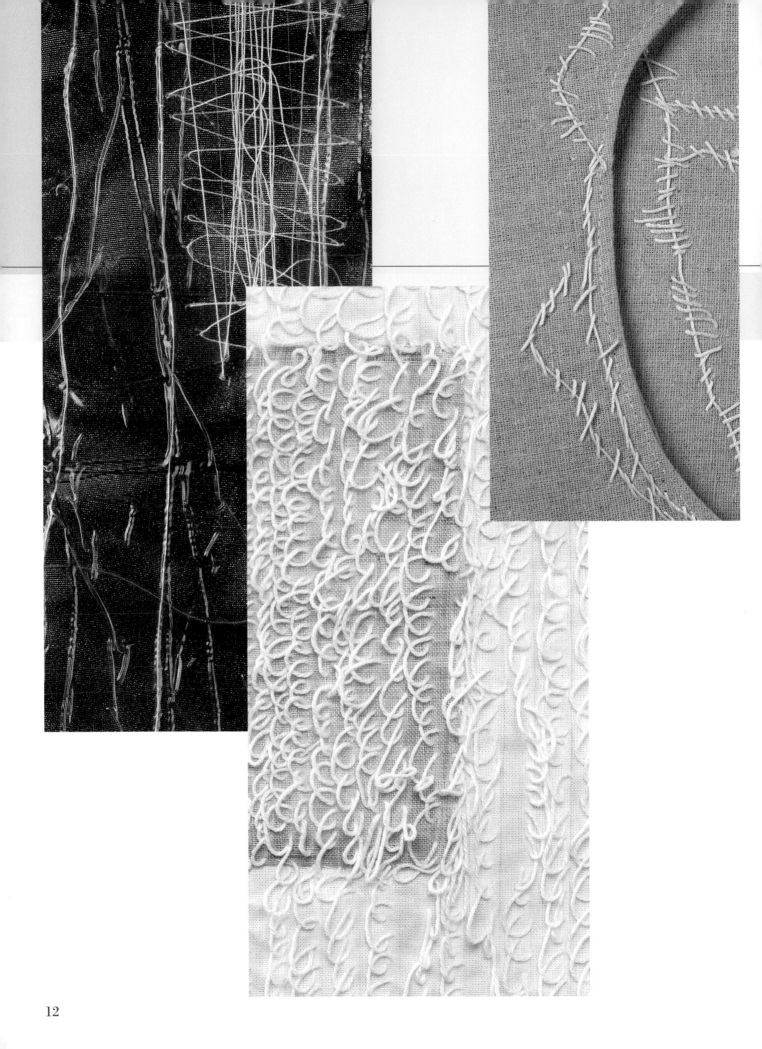

Part One:

Fabrics from Strands

In this section, you will learn how to create cutting-edge fabrics using common household items like electrical tape, packing tape, tissue paper and plastic bags. You'll also discover new and innovative ways to manipulate pre-existing fabrics and sewing-project scraps, such as leftover thread.

The creation of these textural and unexpected surfaces will get your creative juices flowing. If you are a hand stitcher and enjoy direct interaction with the fabric and thread, you'll find some loose and funky things to try, too. If you are the tacky-glue, sticky sort, then you're also in luck. And if you are like me, a mixed-media gal, then you will want to try every fabric featured here and come up with your own creative variations on each one. So, forget the rules; we're not just going to bend them, we're going to break them. Above all, we're going to have some fun.

Bag Puff

A background in theater taught me to use any material to get the desired effect. So, sewing with reclaimed plastic bags wasn't a big jump. I love that when stitching with this bag "thread," it holds its shape.

Materials

fabric of your choice

water-soluble dressmaker pencil or chalk

straightedge or ruler

plastic bag

scissors or rotary cutter

cutting mat

large-eye needle

1 Mark material

Use a water-soluble dressmaker pencil or chalk and a straight-edge to mark straight lines on the fabric. Place these as close together or as far apart as you'd like.

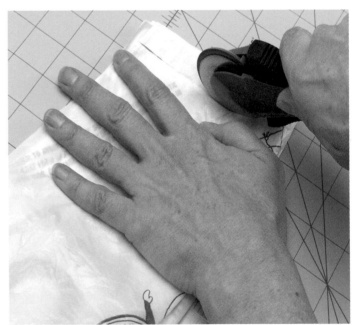

2 Cut strips

Fold a plastic bag in half, across the width of the opening. Use scissors or a rotary cutter to cut ½" (1cm) strips, parallel with the line of the opening.

3 Weather plastic

Thread the first plastic strip from step 2 into the needle. Leave a small tail, approximately 3" (8cm). Insert the needle into your fabric and pull the strip completely through the fabric. This will crinkle the plastic.

4 Create first puff

Insert the needle from the underside of the fabric, coming out on the line drawn in step 1. Leave a 3"–4" (8cm–10cm) tail but don't knot it yet. Backstitch by pushing the needle through to the underside of the fabric 1/8" (3mm) above the thread.

5 Create second puff

Pull the needle on the underside of the fabric until you have a pea-sized puff on the front of the fabric. Insert the needle through the back of the fabric about 1/2" (1cm) below the first puff. Backstitch again as in step 4 to create the second puff. Check the puffs for consistent size. Use a needle to pull the puff out a little and then spread it with your fingers to puff it out, if necessary. Continue making puffs along the line. As you go, hold the plastic taut on the back each time you insert the needle, or you'll flatten the puffs.

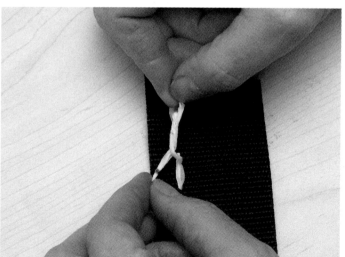

6 Tie ends

Use a new piece of plastic thread when the plastic has gotten too worn or won't puff to the desired size. Tie the tails of the plastic threads together on the underside of the fabric.

Loose Threads

When creating bag puffs, be mindful of the base fabric. If the weave of the fabric is too tight, the plastic will break when you pull it through. For this reason, be wary of knits and, instead, look for loose-weave fabrics.

Paper Fabric

Years ago in South Korea, I watched a television show instructing viewers how to create paper fabric by weaving with rice paper. I was fascinated that something seemingly so fragile could produce something so sturdy.

I later developed my own version of paper fabric, balancing strong threads and fragile tissue paper—simple ingredients yielding a complex structure.

Materials

tissue paper in various colors

plastic garbage bag (to protect your work surface)

water

all-purpose glue

paintbrush

crochet thread and scrap threads

texturizing items (bamboo skewer shreds, leaves, paper bits, etc.)

sewing thread

1 Apply glue to first layer of paper

Lay out plastic bag over your work surface. Place tissue paper waxy side down onto the plastic. Add a little water to the glue. Apply a thin layer of glue to the tissue paper.

2 Add texture

Cut about a 4' (1m) length of crochet thread. Randomly layer the crochet thread and scrap threads onto the tissue paper while the adhesive is still wet.

To add extra texture, include bamboo skewers, leaves, small bits of paper—anything that you want—onto your tissue paper.

3 Add structure

Apply sewing thread in horizontal and vertical rows to add stability to the paper.

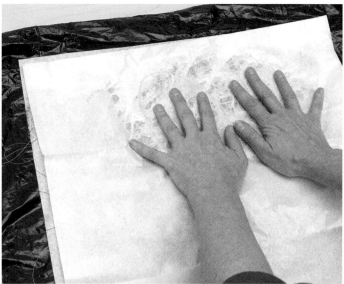

4 Add second layer of paper

Apply another layer of tissue paper and press firmly to sandwich the threads.

5 Apply more glue

Use a paintbrush to apply a layer of glue to the second layer of paper.

6 Apply additional layers

Vary the colors of the tissue paper and threads and repeat the entire process as many times as desired for the effect you want. Feel free to experiment with adhesives, finishes and materials.

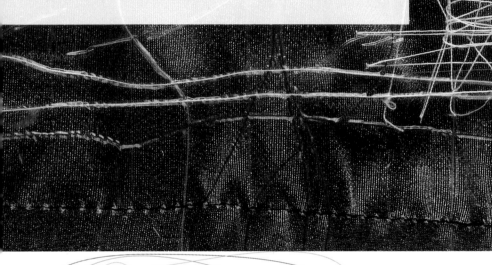

Thread and Tape

The most common misperception of fabric is that it has to be either woven or knit, but there are many fabrics that are neither. Nonwoven fabrics are broadly defined as structures bonded together by entangling fiber or filaments. Flat sheets are made from separate fibers or from molten plastic or plastic film. Here, packing tape acts as the bonding agent, while overlapping fibers add stability and work as a design element. You can vary the amount of tape, fiber or plastic.

Materials

soft plastic (garbage bag, grocery bag, plastic wrap, caution tape, etc.)

double-sided tape

sewing thread

silver or gold leaf sheets (optional)

packing tape (thinnest is best)

scissors

electrical tape (optional)

crochet thread

Loose Threads

If you want to strengthen the fabric or just add more texture without adding color, use a color of thread that is the same color as the plastic.

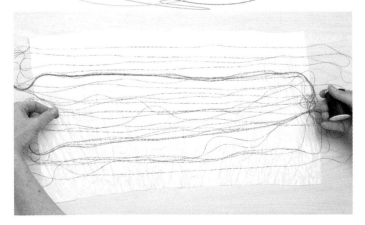

1 Lay first layer of thread

Cut the bag apart and spread one layer of it as large as possible. Place double-sided tape at the edges of the plastic. Lay first layer of thread horizontally across the plastic, using the tape to hold it in place.

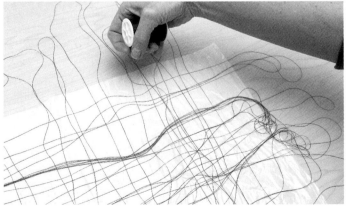

2 Add second layer of thread

Add a layer of threads running vertically over the first layer. You can add the silver or gold leafing during any of the layers.

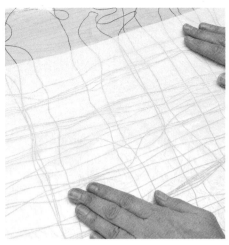

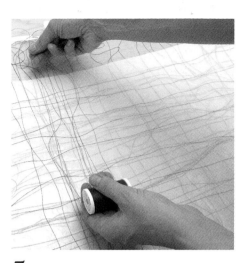

3 Apply packing tape

Cut strips of packing tape that are a little longer than the width of the plastic. Lay the packing tape horizontally across the plastic. You need only a few strips to stabilize the plastic. Apply another layer of packing tape in vertical strips, completely covering the plastic and thread.

4 Add texture

Flip the piece over, packing-tape side down. Rub your hands over the entire piece to get the threads to stand out and show texture.

5 Create double-sided fabric (optional)

With the fabric still laying packing-tape side down, repeat steps 1–4. Feel free to use different colors of thread and add more layers of packing tape to add texture and color to the fabric.

Variations

Here are some different things to do with the thread. It can be snipped and sprinkled or loosely arranged, and electrical tape can replace packing tape.

Cut-thread fabric

Electrical-tape fabric

1 Apply cut-thread

Lay plastic over your work surface as you did for step 1. Instead of laying the thread in rows, bunch it in your hand and cut tiny pieces of thread over the plastic.

1 Apply thread and tape

Lay a heavier thread (such as crochet thread) on the plastic, in a random, pattern (don't worry about rows). Gently pull small pieces of electrical tape off of the roll (stretching it may keep it from laying flat), and lay the tape over the thread and plastic, slightly overlapping the tape strips. Flip over and rub plastic over thread to remove any bubbles and add texture.

Thread Ball

I love tearing fabric, and the by-product of this process is thread. Because of my love of this process, I had thread everywhere. Then, one day I had that "what-if" moment and rolled the threads to create this wonderful color ball. It was no longer garbage.

I continued making them, still unsure what I was going to do with them. An idea came to me—a necklace, a beautiful, colored-thread necklace (see page 56). As you will see in chapter 2, there are many different ways to wear these little gems!

Materials

crochet thread in 2 colors

scissors

large-eye needle

1 Pile yarn

Use scissors to cut a length of crochet thread. A 3' (1m) length will result in a ½" (1cm) ball. Adjust this as desired. Loosely gather the crochet thread in your hand.

2 Turn and fold

Turn the ball clockwise and fold it on itself. Repeat folding it on itself until it's as small and tight as possible.

3 Add second thread

Insert approximately 30" (76cm) of a second color of crochet thread into a needle. Insert the needle into the center of the ball. Pull the needle through the ball, leaving a 6" (15cm) tail of thread.

4 Wrap ball

Hold the tail for tension and maneuverability. With your other hand, wrap the remaining crochet thread around the center of the ball three times.

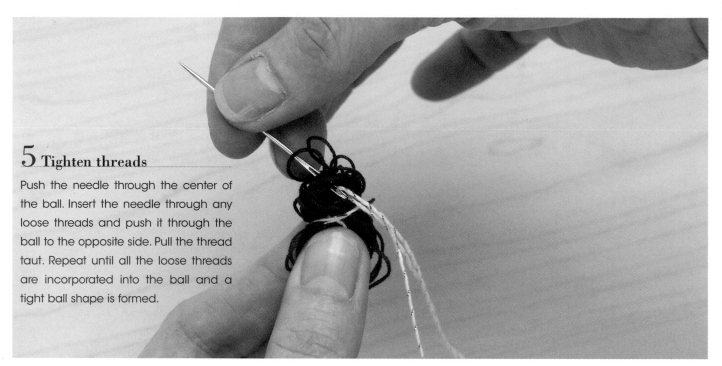

5 Tighten threads

Push the needle through the center of the ball. Insert the needle through any loose threads and push it through the ball to the opposite side. Pull the thread taut. Repeat until all the loose threads are incorporated into the ball and a tight ball shape is formed.

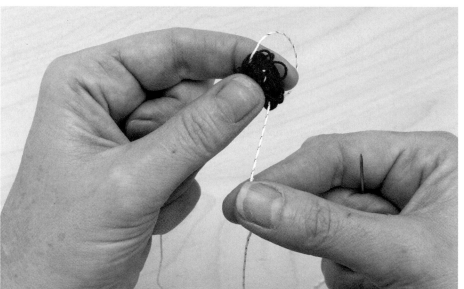

6 Wrap second color

Wrap the thread around the ball to insert the needle on the bottom of the ball, directly under the thread from step 5. Repeat steps 5–6 until the ball is firmly shaped and the second color of thread looks good.

7 Cut thread

Leave a tail on the ball for attaching the thread ball to the project of your choice.

Loop-to-Loop

I wanted to create a fabric that had some tactile texture and some rise to it. My daughter said, "You know, Mom, Velcro is a fabric." This simple loop-to-loop stitch has a simplicity to it, yet the possibilities are endless: Change the color, size and number of strands of the thread; experiment with the base fabric, choosing similar colors or contrasting ones; vary the space between the stitches, the height of the stitches, the space between the rows of stitches . . . the variations are endless.

Materials

fabric

water-soluble dressmaker pencil

straightedge or ruler

crochet thread

scissors

large-eye needle

1 Make guidelines

Use a straightedge or ruler and a water-soluble dressmaker pencil to draw a straight line across the fabric. Place a mark every ½" (1cm) onto the fabric.

2 Start first stitch

Cut crochet thread to a length of 18" (46cm). Insert thread into a needle. Knot the end of the thread. Insert the needle from the underside of the fabric through the first mark made in step 1, about ½" (1cm) from the edge, and pull taut. Then insert the needle ¼" (6mm) closer to the edge of the fabric and push it through to the underside of the fabric. Don't pull the thread yet.

3 Finish first stitch

Push the needle through the front side of the fabric ¾" (2cm) from the edge or ¼" (6mm) to the left of where you first inserted the thread in step 1. Don't pull the thread taut.

Loose Threads

I used a fabric with a fringed edge, but you can quickly create a ½" (1cm) finished edge by rolling the edge in ¼" (6mm) two times and straight stitching a quick hem.

4 Shape loop

Using your thumb as a stopper, pull the thread until it hits your thumb, creating the size of the loop that you want. Adjust the loop size as desired by pulling on the thread to loosen it or pulling on the needle to tighten it.

5 Start second stitch

Push the needle through the front side of the fabric in the center of the loop created in step 4.

6 Finish second stitch

Remaining on the marked line, push the needle through to the front side of the fabric ¼" (6mm) to the left of the thread from step 3.

7 Shape second loop

Place your thumb in the center of where the second loop will be, and pull the thread as you did in step 4 to create the second loop.

When pushing the needle through to the underside of the fabric, avoid going through the threads that are on the underside, or you'll pull the loops too taut.

8 Continue stitching

Push the needle through the front side of the fabric in the center of the second loop as you did in steps 5 and 6. Shape the third loop as you did in step 4. Continue creating loops for the entire row.

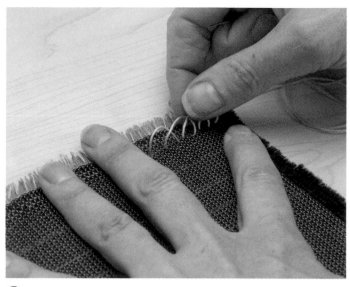

9 Shape loops

As you sew, stop occasionally to pull and adjust the loops to make them all a uniform size.

10 Start second row

Insert the needle in the front side of the fabric in the center of the last loop on the first row. From the underside of the fabric, push the needle through to the front of the fabric, directly below the center of the last loop from the first row. Make sure to keep the loose thread above the stitches you're making.

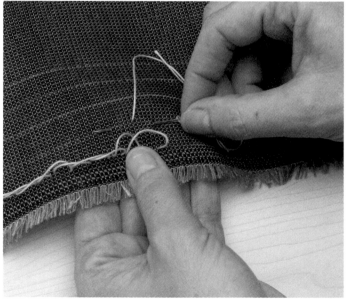

11 Start second stitch

Rotate the fabric 180 degrees, keeping the front side up, and repeat steps 2–9 for the next row, working from right to left.

Loose Thread

Gather thread scraps into piles, sorting them by color, texture or by fabric type. Loose thread creates such wonderful texture. And by using it, you're truly making an upcycled fabric. (Loose thread from taffeta doesn't play well with other threads. Threads from fabrics that resemble standard sewing thread work best.)

Materials

fabric

sewing thread scraps (balled up bundles are fine)

sewing thread

sewing machine

scissors

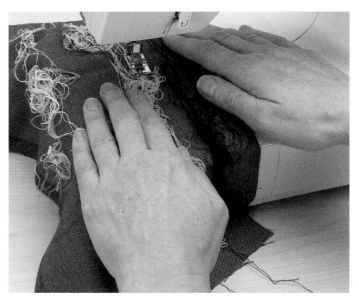

1 Lay thread

Choose colors and thickness of threads that will achieve your desired effect. Slightly separate knotted balls of thread with your fingers, but it's OK to leave it somewhat tangled. Lay the threads on the fabric randomly, as though you're painting abstractly with the thread.

2 Sew threads to fabric

Using a sewing machine and thread of any type and color, and any type of stitches, secure the loose threads to the fabric. Repeat with as many or as few colors of thread as desired. Be sure to trim the threads from the sewing machine close to the fabric. The only loose threads here should be intentional.

Scribble

A simple way to create texture, color and pattern, this quick and easy stitch will change any base fabric from an ordinary one to an eyecatching piece of art. Go bold with contrasting colors and strong designs or more reserved with thread that's the same color as the fabric. Either way, have fun! Start with an existing design, or, if you're the adventurous type, just start sewing without a drawn pattern. What's most important is to get started!

Materials

fabric

crochet thread

large-eye needle

scissors

water-soluble dressmaker pencil (optional)

1 Sketch design (Optional)

If you'd like, use a water-soluble dressmaker pencil to create the design that you will "scribble" stitches over.

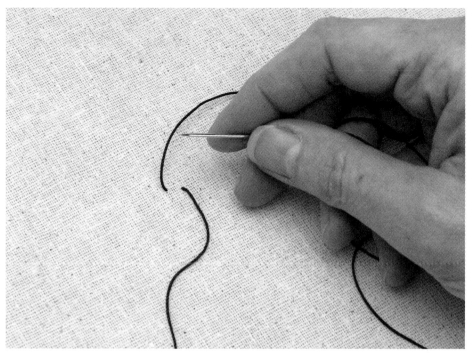

2 Create anchor

Insert crochet thread into a needle. Knot the end of the crochet thread. Insert the crochet thread through the underside of the fabric at the beginning of the line drawn in step 1 (or wherever you wish to freehand the start of the stitches). Then push the needle through the front side of the fabric at a point far from where the thread first came through the fabric, creating a long line of thread. The long line is your anchor and can be any length you like—typically between 3" and 6" (7cm and 15cm). Thread the needle again from the back to the front, just slightly to the side of where it just passed through the fabric.

3 Secure anchor thread

When the anchor is the length you want, start to create stitches that cross over the anchor, using various lengths and widths. This can be very asymmetrical.

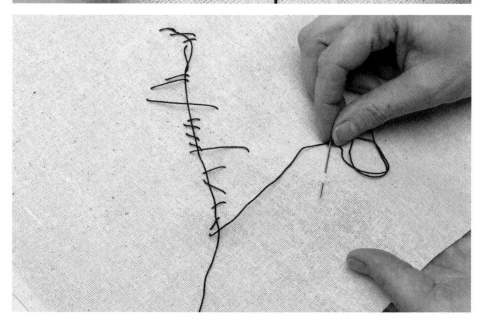

4 Continue with design

Expand upon your design by taking the thread and creating new anchors. Make circles or whatever strikes your fancy. When you've completed your design, knot the thread on the underside of the fabric and cut thread.

Seam Allowance

I like the look of both serged and raw edges, so I decided to create a fabric of exposed seams. You can easily accomplish this look, too, either by sewing functional seams on the correct side of the fabric or by creating faux seams. This technique works great for fabric that is really cool on both sides. If you want the seams to lay flat, iron them out or simply topstitch them in place.

Materials

fabric

sewing thread

straightedge or ruler

rotary cutter

cutting mat

sewing machine

Faux Seam

A faux seam allows you to quickly add texture to any garment by attaching a strip of material to a finished piece.

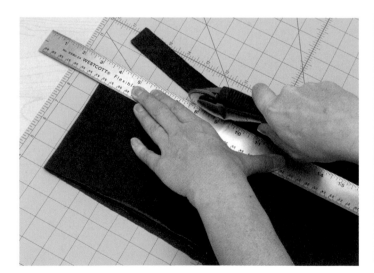

1 Cut strips for seam allowance

Lay the fabric onto a cutting mat. Using a straightedge on the fabric as a guide, cut a 1" (3cm) strip from the fabric. Repeat for as many seams as you want exposed.

2 Sew your seam

Use a sewing machine to straight stitch a line down the center of one layer of the strip. Add as many additional strips as you like, connecting them as you go.

Materials

fabric

pins

sewing thread

sewing machine

iron

Visible Seam Allowance

The fabric for the visible seam allowance can have two visibly distinct tones of color on each side or use two colors of fabric.

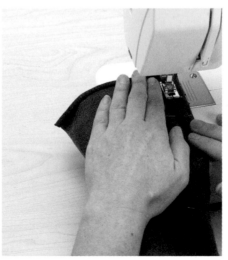

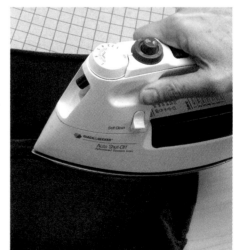

1 Pin fabrics together

Lay fabric so you have one right side and one wrong side together. Use pins to secure.

2 Sew seam

Place the piece from step 1 in the sewing machine with the edges of the fabric lined up with the seam-allowance line, usually ⅝" (2cm) to the right of the presser foot. Straight stitch the seam.

3 Press seam

Using an iron, press seam open on the outside of the fabric.

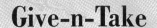

Give-n-Take

During the Elizabethan period, dressmakers would slash the ornate brocade outer-garment, then pull the white undershirt through the slit so it created a white puff. This fabric takes this process a step farther and uses the cut-out pieces as added decorative and textural elements.

This is another great way to use your scraps from other projects and create new fabrics by mixing patterns or color.

Materials

fabric

water-soluble dressmaker pencil (optional)

rotary cutter

cutting mat

precison-tip scissors

sewing thread

sewing machine

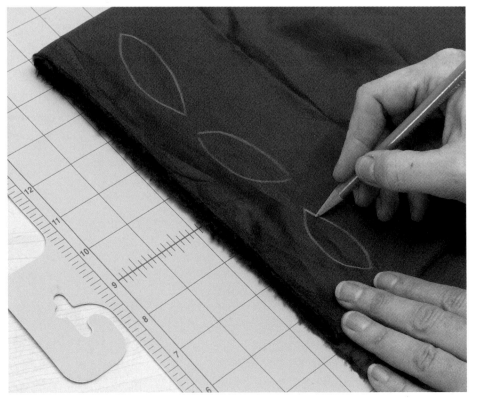

1 Create shapes in fabric

Measure the fabric to the desired size. Fold the fabric multiple times, leaving about 2" (5cm) on each edge for finishing. Use a water-soluble dressmaker pencil to create shapes 2" (5cm) along the edge of the fabric, or to sketch freeform designs of your own.

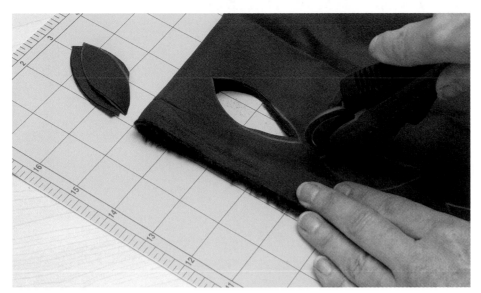

2 Cut designs from fabric

Use a rotary cutter on its heaviest setting and cut out the marked shapes. If the rotary cutter doesn't completely cut through all of the layers, use small, sharp scissors to cut out the rest.

3 Stabilize cutouts

Use your sewing machine to straight stitch around the cutouts. Don't worry about straight lines or precision. These stitches stabilize the cutouts and add a decorative element. Repeat 2–3 times with the same or different color of thread.

4 Add cutouts

Take your cutouts from step 2 and place them along the fabric. Straight stitch them in place. Here I'm decoratively stitching down the center to create the center vein of the leaf.

Loose Threads

You can use use the positive or the negative space of this project. See the scarflet (page 102) and the apron (page 51) for examples of these.

Part Two:

Projects from Fabrics

Now that we have made these incredible fabrics, what do we do with them? While they are wall-art worthy, we can have some real fun making wearable art from our fabric creations.

In Chapter 1, we'll start out with some simple and straightforward clothing items that are easy and fun to make. The Marks Dress is a simple, muslin tank dress that focuses on the scribble fabric as a wonderful, yet simple, texture. Explore the options of using thread the same color as the muslin, or make a bold statement with a contrasting thread. The Upcycled Apron (see page 50), showcasing loose threads, is both functional and stylish. Why not customize and entire outfit? With a little planning, you could coordinate the Inside-Out Shirt with the Peekaboo Skirt for a unique look from head to toe.

In Chapter 2 we'll transform textile creations into jewelry you create with your own special signature. Some pieces, like the Smidgen Ball Necklace (see page 57) are make-and-go and can even serve as last-minute gifts. Others, like the Pulp-Wear Cuff (see page 61) will need a bit more time to complete.

Then, in Chapter 3, it's time to accessorize in style! Whether your preference is for pulp or puff, we have you covered here. Dress up any outfit with the Remnants Belt (see page 84), or keep it casual with an earth-friendly alternative (see page 98). And just imagine creating a different clutch (see page 90) for every pair of shoes!

Finally, in Chapter 4, you'll find outerwear designs that can be as hot and haute as you wish to make them. Whether you prefer a cape (see page 108) or a shawl (see page 114), your choices of color and texture will have you wearing either with pizzazz.

The items you create will be pieces of art. Take great pleasure in the process of creating these one-of-a-kind wearables. Life doesn't need to be difficult, and neither does art—or style!

CHAPTER 1

Clothes

The clothes in this chapter possess cool elegance and style, yet there are no difficult sewing techniques to learn—you get to go straight to the fun part—decorating and wearing!

Scribble stitching, two-toned fabrics, cut-out shapes and more are just the start, so jump in with both feet and craft your one-of-a-kind item for that special occasion that's always just around the corner.

Inside-Out Shirt

This shirt is created from a simple pattern. For my version, I chose a cotton-Lycra blend, which stretches in all directions. For your own shirt, consider using a two-toned fabric: It will create wonderful texture and patterns when it is combined with the Seam-Allowance technique. Remember, both sides of your fabric will be showcased.

Featured Fabric: Seam Allowance (see page 30).

Materials

fabric, two-toned knit, 2 panels 18" × 25" (46cm × 64cm) for size 8 (Adjust amount as needed.)

copy of shirt pattern (see page 118)

scissors

cutting mat (optional)

water-soluble dressmaker pencil

pins

sewing thread

sewing machine

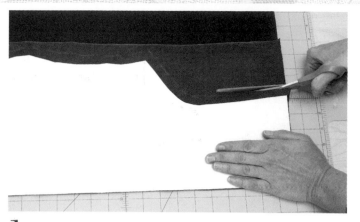

1 Cut fabric

For the top portion of the shirt, cut fabric to 20" × 17" (51cm × 43cm) or to the dimensions needed for your adjusted size. The lighter-toned side of the fabric (usually the underside) is the "right side" for this shirt. With the fabric folded, lay the pattern (pages 118–119) on the fold. Cut the pattern from the fabric, allowing room for a ½" (1cm) seam allowance on the cut side. Fold the fabric again and cut out the second pattern piece. Use a water-soluble dressmaker pencil to mark the bottom of the armhole so you don't accidentally sew through it.

2 Cut the waistband

Cut two strips of fabric to 6½" × 17" (17cm × 43cm) or to the dimensions needed for your adjusted size. The darker-toned side will be the "right side" for the waistband.

Loose Threads

Check how long you want your shirt to be and adjust the seam allowance to fit your needs. Before you cut, you might want to add your seam allowance with a water-soluble dressmaker pencil, just to mark where you will be cutting.

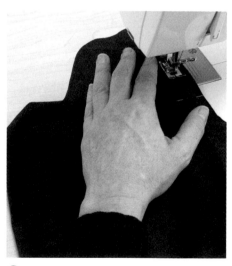

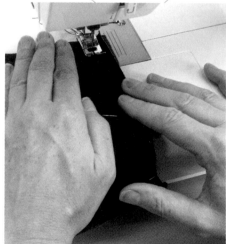

3 Sew shirt

Pin shirt pieces with right sides together. Sew a ½" (1cm) seam allowance from the neck to the top of the shoulder. Backstitch to secure. Cut the thread. Sew a ½" (1cm) seam starting at the bottom mark of the armhole to the bottom of the shirt. Backstitch to secure. Cut the threads.

4 Finish armholes

Turn the armhole edges in ¼" (6mm) and pin. Straight stitch the edge to finish. Cut the threads.

5 Create waistband

Pin the waistband pieces with the wrong sides together. Sew a ½" (1cm) seam at each end of the waistband to form a complete circle. Cut the threads.

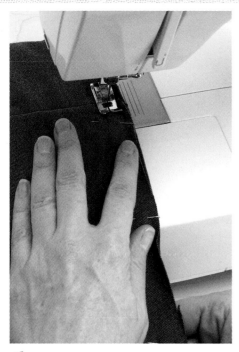

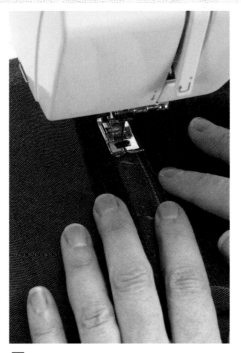

6 Attach waistband to shirt

Turn the top right-side out. Pin the waist-band to the shirt with the waistband's light side against the shirt's dark side. This will create the visible seam allowances. (See detail shot at right.)

7 Secure seam allowance (optional)

Topstitch the visible seam allowance (where the shirt and waistband meet) to prevent rolling, if desired.

Detail

This shirt gets its personality from the deliberate and visible seams.

Variations

It's easy to add visible seams when making a dress. You can use any dress pattern or try the Marks dress pattern (page 46) and sew one, two or all of the seams with the allowance on the outside. Here, I used both seam allowance techniques to create this dress. The seams under the bust and down the center of the front and back of the dress are all seams with the allowance on the outside. (A bonus to the center seams is that you can adjust the size of the dress by adjusting the size of these allowances.) The two seams at the bottom are fake (page 30). Use this inside-out seam allowance technique anytime you want to add texture to a garment.

Peekaboo Skirt

Wraparound skirts are simple and adjustable, and they perform a nice little flap number when you walk. Adjust the tie on this skirt to fit your style—a little longer for wrapping, tying into a big bow or tying into a half bow with one tie blowing in the wind.

Featured Fabric: Give-and-Take (see page 32).

Materials

textured sheer, 36" × 56" (91cm × 142cm) for size 8, allowing 15" (38cm) of overlap (Adjust amount as needed.)

cotton fabric, 25" × 48" (64cm × 122cm) for size 8, allowing 7½" (19cm) of overlap (Adjust amount as needed.)

scissors

rotary cutter (optional)

cutting mat (optional)

sewing thread

sewing machine

pins

1 Create cut fabric

Cut two pieces of the textured sheer fabric to 4" × 56" (10cm × 142cm) to serve as ties. Fold the remaining sheer fabric length-wise four times. Make cutouts through all four layers of the textured sheer, along the 56" (142cm) length (folded to now be 14" [36cm]), about 1½" (4cm) from all edges and 1½" (4cm) apart. Unfold the fabric and stabilize all of the cutouts by sewing around them (see page 33).

Loose Threads

Adjust the length of this skirt to whatever size you prefer. The instructions here result in a 27" (69cm) length. The easiest way to determine the width you'll need for your particular size, is to measure your waist where you want the skirt to sit, and add 15" (38cm) for the sheer fabric and 7½" (19cm) for the cotton. The dimensions for the ties, as given, should then fit you regardless of you size.

2 Sew lining to skirt

With the wrong side of the cotton against the wrong side of the textured sheer fabric, straight stitch a seam lengthwise along one side for 48" (122cm). You will have 8" (20cm) of the textured sheer fabric remaining.

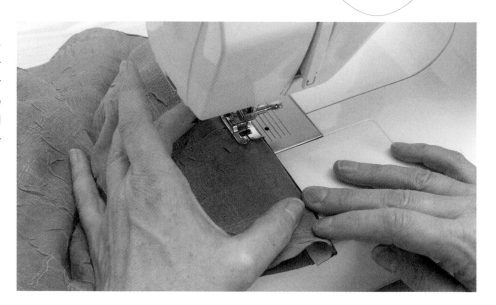

3 Add tie

Fold one piece of the tie material from step 1 lengthwise over the top of the waist on the end that doesn't have the extra sheer material. Straight stitch at 1½" (4cm) to secure.

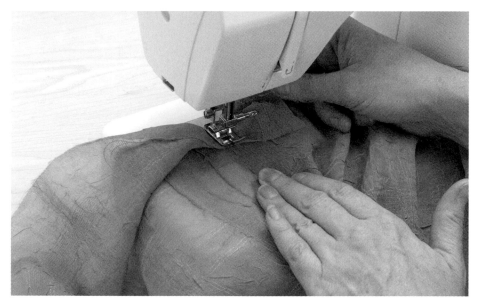

4 Add other tie

Bunch the loose sheer material on the end of the waist. Secure the sheer material to the skirt by straight stitching at ¼" (6mm). Be sure that you sew through both the sheer and cotton layers.

Loose Threads

When the skirt is too small, your whole thigh shows when you walk and even more when you sit. When you are measuring the widest part of your hips, just add another 8" (20cm) or so. Before you cut the fabric, walk around in it and see if there is enough fabric for your comfort zone. The length of this skirt is up to you. Look in the mirror and slowly move the length up or down, keeping in mind there is a cutout section running along the bottom of the skirt.

Marks Dress

Designers will often use muslin to mock up a new design. After they've made all their corrections and adjustments, they take it apart, create a pattern from it and cut out the garment from a "real" fabric. Muslin is reminiscent of linen, but much more forgiving when it comes to wrinkles, making it a "real" fabric in my book. The crisp and natural feeling of muslin brings to mind a fresh spring day. Using natural crochet thread and the Scribble stitch adds to the organic feel of this project.

Featured Fabric: Scribble (see page 28).

Materials

soft-grade muslin, 2 panels 30" × 35" (76cm × 89cm) for size 8 (Adjust accordingly for desired length and fullness.)

copy of dress pattern (see page 121)

pins

scissors

water-sluble dressmaker pencil

sewing thread

large-eye needle

sewing machine

un-dyed crochet thread

transfer paper (optional)

1 Cut fabric

Fold one piece of muslin in half so that the fold is 35" (89cm) long. Pin the pattern (page 121) onto the fold. Use a water-soluble dressmaker pencil to mark the pattern markings. The pattern ends at the natural waist, so continue down the remainder of the panel with the fullness you desire. **Note:** This is a fairly loose pattern and you could easily improvise your own if desired. While this dress ends up being 34" (86cm) in length, start with a larger panel, if you desire a longer dress.

2 Sew seams

Pin the cut pieces with right sides together. Sew the side and shoulder seams at the seam allowance line, usually ⅝" (2cm).

Loose Threads

This muslin has a semi-rough hand to it and is medium weight. Its natural color is also opaque.

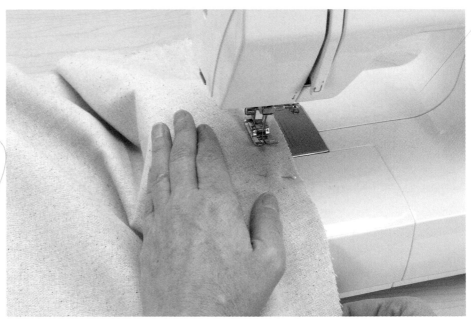

3 Sew arm hems

Create a ½" (1cm) hem by folding the armholes in ¼" (6mm) twice. Pin and straight stitch the edges to finish.

Loose Threads

The neck and arm openings of this dress are a bit larger than normal so that tanks or T-shirts can be worn underneath for a layered ook.

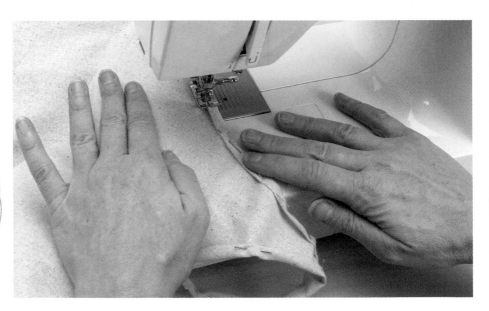

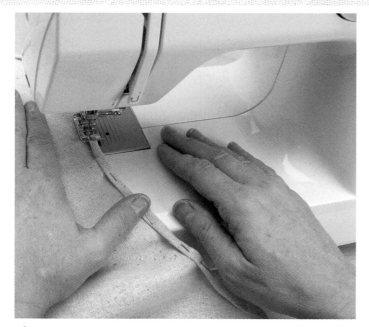

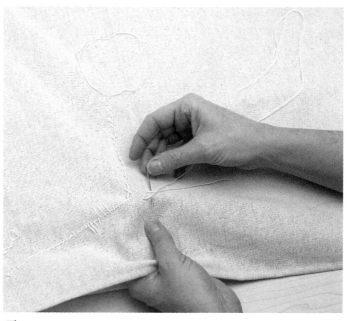

4 Sew neck and bottom hems

Create a ½" (1cm) hem by folding the neckline and the bottom hem in ¼" (6mm) twice. Pin and straight stitch the edges to complete.

5 Apply hand-stitching to dress

Scribble (page 28) a freeform design onto the dress or use transfer paper to apply the design featured here (page 121) or your own design.

Variations

Adding a scribble to purchased items adds texture and dimension, taking any ordinary piece to extraordinary. The scribble stitch easily lends itself to store-bought items, and it adds a personalized touch.

This cap and clutch were purchased items. For both of them, I chose black and stitched with rainbow crochet thread. Or like the scribble dress, you can go subtler and use the same color thread to create a wonderful detail. As for the skirt, I made a simple tube skirt with an elastic waist and used a similar color thread. At first you don't notice it—it's just a subtle layer of texture.

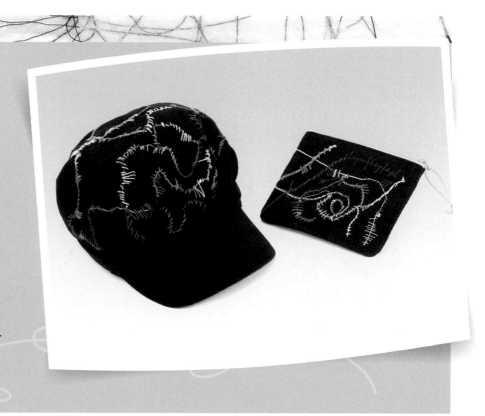

Upcycled Apron

Feel free to sashay through the kitchen in this apron, but keep in mind that it has awesome potential beyond the culinary variety. Wear it as an accessory over jeans, skirts and dresses. The suit fabric juxtaposes perfectly with the texture of the loose threads. This apron is really one-size-fits-all, but ideally, it should wrap around your hips. When you twirl around, the big sheer bow and long ties fly in the breeze like a wake from a boat. You'll be an eyecatcher coming and going.

Featured Fabric: Loose Thread (see page 27).

Materials

suit fabric, 18" × 35" (46cm × 89cm) (Finished apron is approximately 32" [81cm] wide and 16" [41cm] long, without the ties.)

sheer fabric 4½" × 87" (11cm × 221cm)

sewing thread

sewing machine

loose threads

scissors

pins

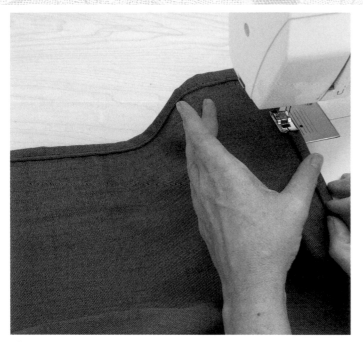

1 Create hems

Fold in the side edges of the suit fabric ½" (1cm) twice, and straight stitch to secure. Repeat for the bottom edge.

2 Create design with thread

Spread loose threads along the bottom edge of the apron in a band approximately 1½" (4cm) wide.

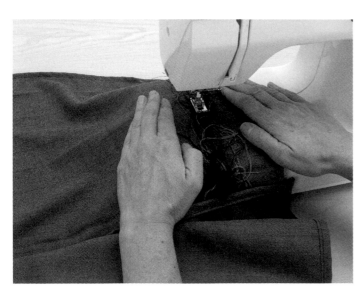

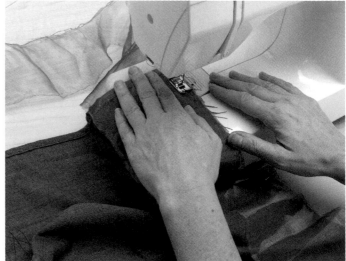

3 Sew loose threads

Randomly sew the loose threads to secure them to the fabric. If any threads get caught around the presser foot, just cut them.

4 Attach tie

Align the edge of the 4½" × 87" (11cm × 221cm) sheer fabric strip with the top edge of the back of the apron. Pin together and straight stitch the tie to the apron with the presser foot running along the edge of the apron.

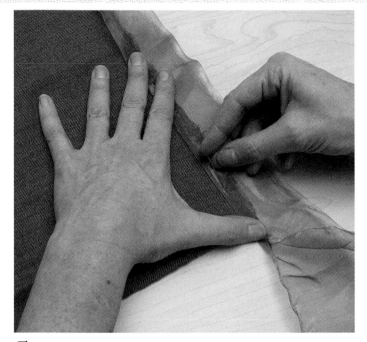

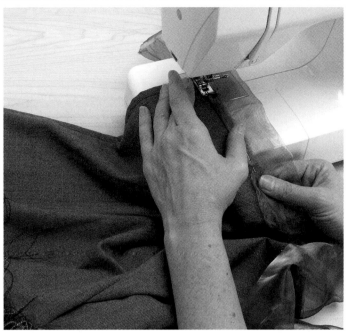

5 Fold and pin tie

Fold the sheer strip toward the front. Push the seam allowance up. On the left side of the apron, fold the edge of the tie in half and pin it at the end. Continue to fold and pin until you get to the edge of the apron material.

6 Finish tie edge

If you have a lot of loose threads on the seam allowance, trim them now. Otherwise, you may sew them into the edge and let them show through the tie. Fold the top edge of the tie down ½" (1cm), then fold the tie over to sew the folded edge to the top portion of the seam allowance.

Variations

While the apron is sophisticated and the scarflet fun and edgy, the technique is the same—loose thread. With the apron, you sew the loose threads on after the apron has been created, but when creating the scarflet, you should stitch the threads onto the cut red taffeta before sewing the scarf together with the plaid fabric. This allows you to keep the plaid fabric clean of stitches. Try creating an abstract landscape with the loose threads for more visual appeal.

CHAPTER 2

Jewelry

Thread as texture is really the star in this chapter. From thread balls to thread loops to random swirls of thread lines—each and every one creates the "wow" factor. Whether it's a single thread ball for a dramatic feel or a resourceful use of your scraps from the last chapter, all of these projects have a playful attitude. And who says jewelry has to be uncomfortable? The Grass Roots Pendant (see page 64) is so light you'll forget you're wearing it. And the Dewey-Decimal Pendant (see page 76) proves that it is possible to have your stitch and wear it too.

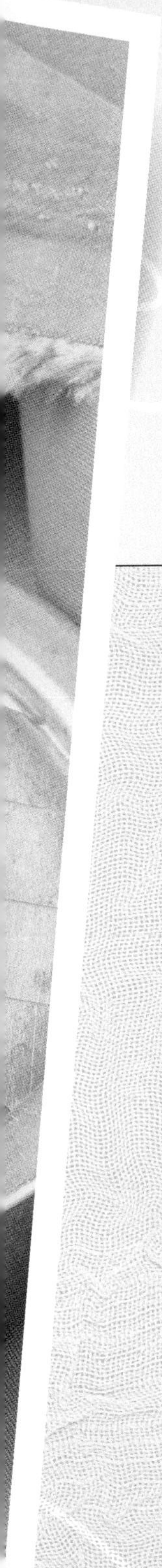

Smidgen Ball Necklace

Sometimes less is more. For a simple yet dramatic focal point, why not give a solitary thread ball a whirl? You can make it monochromatic, or mix it up with any color combination. The accompanying chain allows you to either dress it up or down. This is an easy make-and-go necklace to wear or give as a last-minute gift.

Featured Fabric: Thread Ball (see page 20).

Materials

crochet thread in 2 colors, 3' (1m) each

large-eye needle

scissors

needle-nose pliers

eye pin

jump ring

necklace cord with clasp

1 Start thread ball

Follow the instructions for steps 1–4 on pages 20–21 (though you may omit the long tail mentioned). Use pliers to create a hook in the bottom of the eye pin.

2 Insert eye pin

Push the eye pin into the thread ball, then pull gently so the hook catches the thread ball and only the loop is sticking out.

3 Finish thread ball

Finish making the thread ball, using the instructions for steps 5–7 on page 22. Make sure the eye remains sticking out.

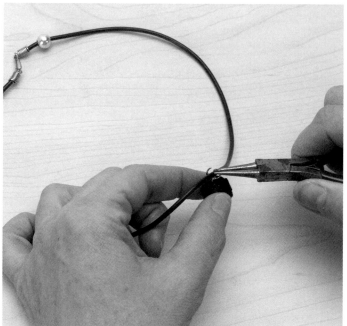

4 Attach to necklace

Insert a jump ring into the loop of the eye pin. Use pliers to attach the jump ring to the necklace cord.

Variations

This ring and the earrings are even easier to make than the Smidgen Ball Necklace, because you don't need to add a wire to the center of the thread ball. When making the ring, check to see what size ball the ring base will hold before creating the thread ball.

When making the earrings, try to create them so they're similar in size and design. Then, simply thread the balls onto a jump ring and attach to a pair of ear wires.

Pulp-Wear Cuff

Imagine how eco-conscious your friends will see you, when you tell

them you made this cuff from paper scraps you almost threw away.

Sometimes the paper we get as junk mail creates the coolest art. You

can play around with the color and size of the paper and thread,

which will create a variety of looks.

Featured Fabric: Paper Fabric (see page 16).

Materials

Paper Fabric, at least 4" × 8" (10cm × 20cm)

pencil

scissors

sewing thread

sewing machine

all-purpose glue

water

tissue paper

paintbrush

crochet thread scraps

hole punch

heavy duty snap kit

water-based dimensional adhesive

1 Cut cuff from fabric

Create paper fabric, according to the instructions on pages 16–17. Use a pencil to draw the shape for the cuff on the dry paper fabric. Cut the fabric to 4" (10cm) wide and a length to fit around your wrist plus 2" (5cm).

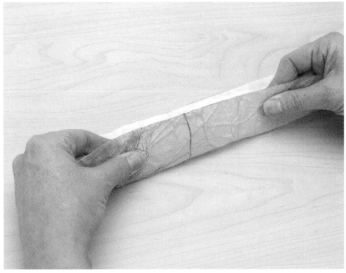

2 Fold cuff

Fold the cuff in half lengthwise to add stability.

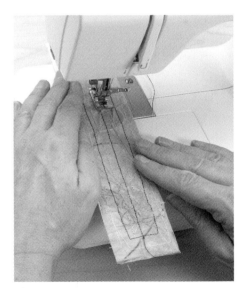

3 Sew cuff edges

Straight stitch around the cuff edges to secure and stabilize the structure. Repeat stitching back and forth a few times with the same or different colored thread down and back up the length of the cuff.

4 Finish edges

Thin glue with a little water. Lay tissue paper on plastic and apply a thin layer of glue. Lay the bracelet onto the glued paper (it doesn't matter which side is facing up; both will be covered). Fold over the sides and secure them with a thin layer of glue.

5 Add threads

Apply a thin layer of glue to one side of the cuff. Take loose threads and create a design on the cuff. Wrap overhanging threads around the side of the cuff and secure with additional glue, or trim off the excess threads when the glue is dry.

6 Create holes for snaps

When the glue is dry, use a pencil to mark where you'd like your snaps to be. I centered the snap cap 1¾" (4cm) from one end and centered the snap receptor at 1¼" (3cm) from the other end. Use a hole punch to create holes at the marks for the snaps.

7 Attach snaps

Make sure you know how to assemble the snap before attaching it to the cuff. Follow the manufacturer's instructions to attach the snaps.

8 Glaze cuff

Apply a thick layer of water-based dimensional adhesive. Spread it evenly across the cuff, but not the snaps. Let one side dry, then repeat on the other side and let it dry.

Variations

Once you've perfected using a snap setter, you can make fun, fashinable cuffs using many of the fabrics in this book, including thread-and-tape, electrical-tape and more.

This thread-and-tape cuff may cause others to slow down and stare. But making it is fast and easy. A few minutes of your time and a few supplies are all you need. Throw caution to the wind and have fun!

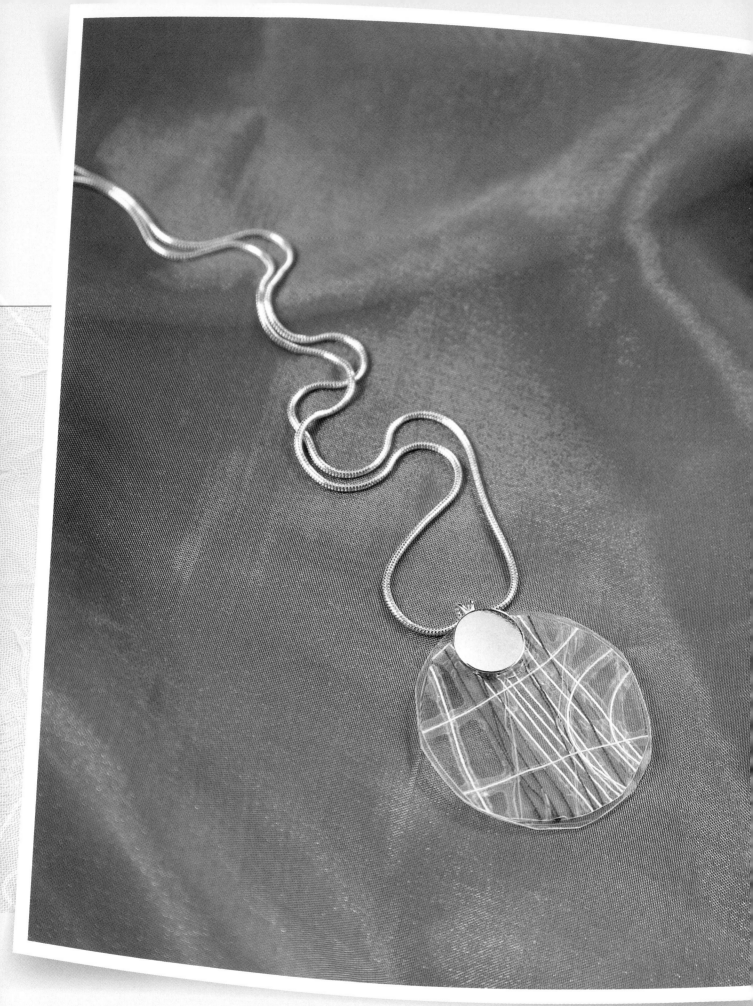

Grass Root Pendant

This beautiful and elegant pendant is awe-inspiring in its simplicity.

There are so many variations that you'll never tire of the options for

combining these simple materials. Explore different shapes, different

colors and different ways to connect them. Make a big sheet of the

basic fabric and then alter the effects for each pendant—they will all

be originals.

Featured Fabric: Thread and Tape (see page 18).

Materials

Thread and Tape Fabric, at least a
2" (5cm) square

pen

plastic template (optional)

thread

packing tape

scissors

pendant disk with bail round, 13mm
silver plate

epoxy

1 Apply design

Find an area of the Thread and Tape fabric that you like. Use a template and a pen to trace the shape you want or draw a shape freehand.

2 Apply second thread

Choose a second color of thread and lay it down just where the shape is traced. Cover with at least two more layers of packing tape for stability.

3 Cut shape

Use the handle of the scissors to burnish the tape and to really get the threads to stand out. Then cut out traced shape.

4 Attach bail

Use epoxy to adhere the pendant to the bail. (Please refer to manufacturer's safety instructions when using this strong adhesive.) Be sure the glue covers the entire bail. While adhesive is still wet, move the pendant to where you want it. Use small clothespins or clamps to apply pressure to the bail and pendant while the adhesive cures.

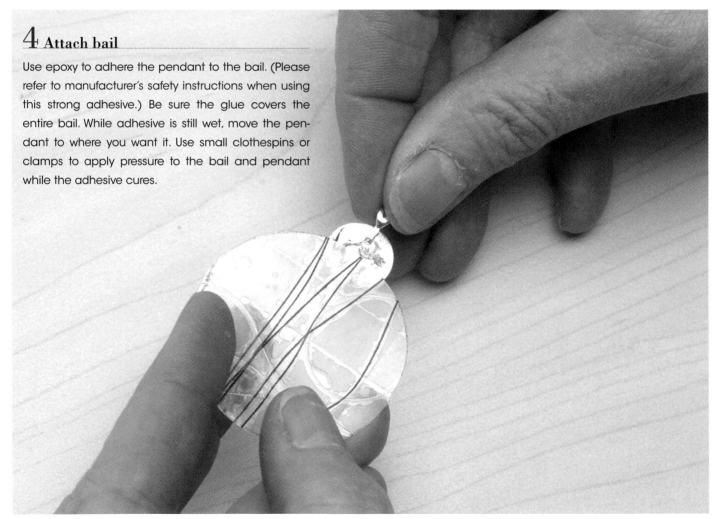

Variations

These variations of the clear disk pendant range from a two-toned disk to beads. Once the fabric has been created from your choice of colors, it is ready to create all of these wonderful accessories. For the disk, I used two different colored circles and made the white circle much smaller than the black one. It was then attached with more packing type. The folded pendant is pretty straightforward. Fold and tape the pendant, leaving an opening for the chain. Decorate as desired.

Making beads requires you to work with small lengths of fabric, about 7" × 3" (18cm × 8cm). The most important thing is to tape down the first part of the roll where the outside of the fabric meets the inside. After it's all taped, continue rolling the fabric nice and tight and then tape down the loose end. Now it is time to cut your beads. Use sharp scissors and cut beads the width you want.

Sparks Ring

What's unusual about Electrical-Tape Fabric is that when you create it, you don't see the final result until you turn it over. The color of the tape and the amount of threads used will both have an impact. Don't stop with a ring; use this fabric to make cool cuff links, tie tacks, hair clips or an edgy pendant.

Featured Fabric: Electrical-Tape Fabric (see page 19).

Materials

Electrical-Tape Fabric, at least a 2" (5cm) square

scissors

button-maker kit for 1" (3cm) buttons

pencil

wire cutters

epoxy

adjustable ring base

1 Cut fabric

Cut a circle of Electrical-Tape Thread Fabric (see page 19) that's slightly larger than the button maker. (See your button-maker kit for details.)

2 Attach button

Place the circle of electrical-tape fabric into a button maker. Press the button top onto the fabric. Fold fabric over the button top. Place a button back over the fabric and button top.

Loose Threads

Electrical tape stretches very easily. So even when you are pulling it from the roll, be careful not to pull it too taut, to prevent wrinkles.

3 Remove shank

Remove the button from the button maker. Use wire cutters to remove the shank from the back of the button.

4 Attach ring

Apply epoxy to the ring base to adhere it to the back of the button. (Please refer to manufacturer's safety instructions when using a strong adhesive.)

Variations

After you've gotten the hang of the button maker, you can create all kinds of accessories that are as cute as a . . . well, you know. Try the bag puff technique using thin strips of electrical tape, then attach the button to a hair clip instead of a ring back. Electrical-Tape Fabric and wire combine to make this edgy choker that's strung on strips of knit fabric.

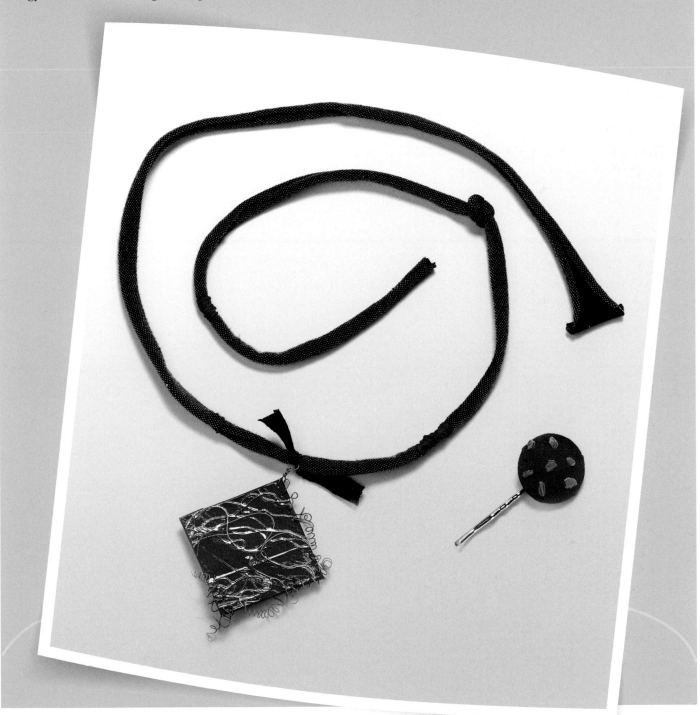

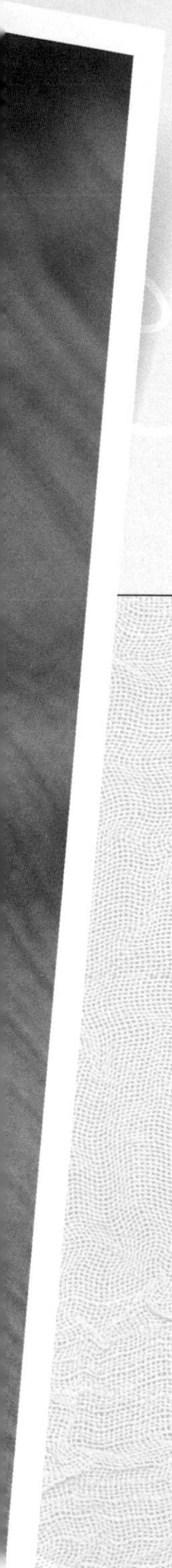

Leftover-Length Ball Necklace

Making thread balls can be addictive. So after making a pile of them, what do you do? Line them up and make a wonderful tactile necklace. You can vary the necklace to your mood or outfit. Add little beads between each ball. Make monochromatic balls for a single-color necklace, or alternate colors. Of course, this look doesn't have to be limited to necklaces. Use stretchy thread and adjust it to be worn as a bracelet.

Featured Fabric: Thread Ball (see page 20).

Materials

thread-balls, various sizes and colors

crochet thread in four colors

large-eye needle

scissors

1 Create design

Create thread balls (see page 20), and cut off the tails from all of them. Lay out the thread balls in your planned design.

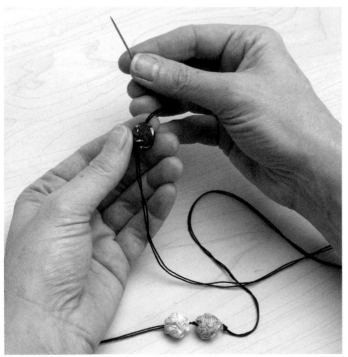

2 Begin stringing thread balls

Cut two strands of crochet thread to a length that's a bit longer than you want the necklace to be. I used two strands cut to 50" (127cm) each. Thread both strands into the needle. Push the needle into the bottom of the first thread ball. Pull needle and thread through. Stop where you want to position the thread ball. Tie a knot after the ball and repeat for as many thread balls as you want on the necklace.

3 Add threads to add length

Insert a second color of thread into the needle and knot the end. Insert the needle through the bottom of the last thread ball (between the last 2 balls and by the last knot). Repeat for the other side. Tie a knot in the threads every 3" (8cm) for the remaining length, to create texture.

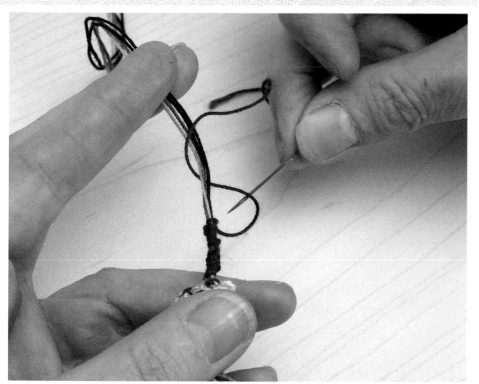

4 Start covering threads

Thread a third color through the end beads. Wrap the threads to create a cord by threading a needle with the fourth color of thread. Anchor the fourth color into the thread ball by inserting the needle on the top of the last ball. Hold the last ball with your thumb and a finger to create tension. Hold the necklace strings taut with two fingers. Create a buttonhole stitch by placing the needle under the group of threads, leaving a loose loop. Run the needle through the loop.

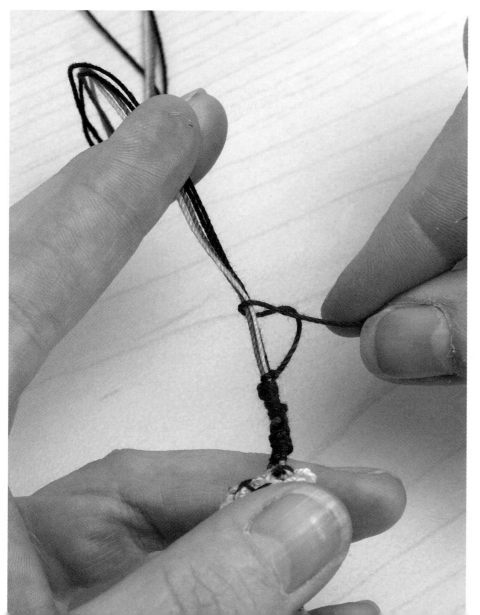

5 Finish covering threads

Pull taut. The buttonhole stitch will twist along the cord as you add more stitches. This is part of the design. Using this stitch, finish covering the threads of the necklace. Tie the cord ends together to join the necklace. You can add a fabric thread ball at the place where you join the cords, if desired.

Dewey-Decimal Pendant

Do more with bookplates than lay claim to your tomes. Instead, make a fashion statement with a couple of bookplates and your custom-made fabrics. This two-sided pendant is a cool and funky way to wear your favorite stitches. Save your test swatches and sandwich two of them between two bookplates—instant, wearable art-to-go.

Featured Fabrics: Bag Puff (see page 14)

Loop-to-Loop (see page 23)

Materials

muslin, 2 3" × 4" (8cm × 10cm) pieces	large-eye needle
	crochet thread
bookplate	fabric glue
bristol board	epoxy
pencil	small clothespins or clamps
scissors	jump rings
water-soluble dress-maker pencil	chain-nose pliers
straight edge or ruler	charm
white plastic bags	bead chain

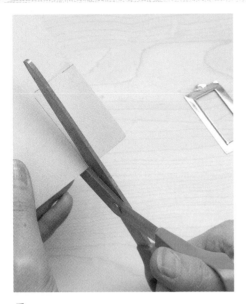

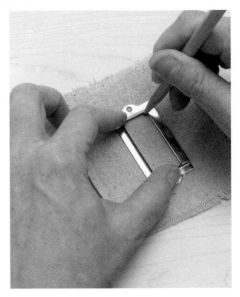

1 Create template

Lay a bookplate on the bristol board, and use a pencil to trace the outside rectangular portion of the bookplate's shape (not the tabs on the ends). Cut inside of the traced line. Trim the cut piece of bristol board as needed so it doesn't show beyond the bookplate edge.

2 Trace template onto muslin

Use a pencil to trace the bristol board template from step 1 onto a piece of 3" × 4" (8cm × 10cm) muslin.

3 Trace inside bookplate

Place the bookplate on the traced musin. Use a pencil to trace the inside of the bookplate. Repeat steps 2–3 for the second piece of muslin.

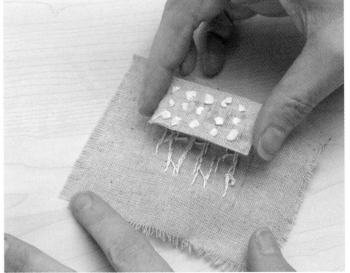

4 Create fabrics and adhere to template

With one piece of the muslin, create Bag-Puff fabric (page 14) within the traced bookplate markings. Now, create Loop-to-Loop fabric (page 23) with the other piece of muslin. Use fabric glue to adhere the bag-puff fabric to the bristol board. Trim the fabric to fit the bristol board.

5 Adhere second fabric to Bristol board

Turn the bristol board over and use the fabric glue to adhere the Loop-to-Loop fabric to the other side of the board.

6 Position the fabric in bookplates

Sandwich the fabric between the bookplates and use E-6000 adhesive to adhere them together. (Please refer to manufacturer's safety instructions when using a strong adhesive.) Make sure the holes on the bookplates line up. Clamp with clothespins to dry.

7 Add jump rings and finish

Using one jump ring, add a charm to the bottom of the book-plate, and with a second jump ring, add a bead chain to the top hole. (Use chain-nose pliers to close both jump rings.) You now have a two-sided pendant—two neckaces in one!

Variations

The bookplate pendant is so versatile. You can choose one or two fabrics to showcase.

When using Bag-Puff fabric, you'll want to decide on the size of the swatch first, and create the bag puffs within the swatch, as I did in this project. Create other fabrics (such as Electical-Tape or Thread and Tape) ahead of time, and just cut them to size. This is a great project for using up your scraps.

Remains-Wrapped Necklace

Repurpose scraps to make this unique necklace. The trick here is to stretch the knit-fabric strips, which causes them to roll onto themselves and become a cord. You can add thread balls, wrap the cord with crochet thread to change the texture, and add colorful elements. Make several necklaces at different lengths, and enjoy these subtle eyecatchers.

Featured Fabric: Thread Ball (see page 20).

Materials

knit fabric strips, various from 14" to 30" × about ¾" (36cm to 76cm × 19mm)

Thread Balls, about 12

scissors

large-eye needle

crochet thread

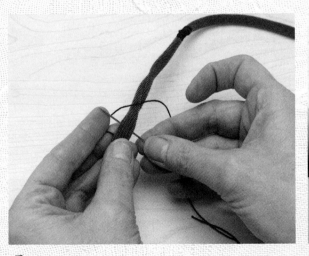

1 Wrap cord

Knot thread and insert it into a needle. Insert the needle through the underside of one piece of the knit fabric. Let the fabric roll back on itself to hide the knot. Begin to wrap the section of fabric by holding the cord between the thumb and fingers and looping the thread to the left of the cord. Then place the needle under the cord and over the thread. Pull taut and continue until the wrap is the desired size.

2 Attach thread balls

Insert the tail of a thread ball (see pages 20–21) into a needle. Push the needle through the underside of the cord fabric. Repeat inserting the needle through the underside of the fabric until you have secured the thread ball. Tie a knot in the cord for texture and to cover where you added the thread ball, if desired.

CHAPTER 3

Accessories

Within this chapter, you'll find an array of projects for your waist, your hand, your wrist, your hair and even a little décor for your keys. From belts to brooch, before heading out, don't forget to accessorize! No matter which of these projects you choose, you're sure to be a showstopper.

Remnants Belt

For this striking number, Thread Fabric is combined with sheer layers to create a sheer-on-sheer effect. It's fun to play with the different tactile qualities and watch how the different fabrics reflect light.

Featured Fabric: Thread and Tape (see page 18).

Loose Threads

There isn't anything special you need to do to sew this plastic fabric, but you do need to be aware that the adhesive from the tape will gunk up your needle. Just stop periodically to clean the needle, and then move on.

Materials

Thread-and-Tape fabric, at least 19½" × 4½" (50cm × 11cm)

muslin, darker shade 4½" × 2" (11cm × 5cm) and small scraps of a lighter shade

sheer fabric, 4½" (11cm) × length to tie around your waist comfortably

rotary cutter

cutting mat

scissors

sewing thread

sewing machine

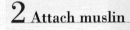

1 Cut Thread-and-Tape fabric

Use a rotary cutter and mat to cut some Thread-and-Tape fabric to 19½" × 4½" (50cm × 11cm).

2 Attach muslin

Cut two small squares (size is up to you) from lighter-toned muslin. Sew the small squares to the piece of darker muslin.

3 Attach ties

Hand stitch the muslin piece from step 2 to the Thread-and-Tape rectangle from step 1. Cut a piece of sheer fabric to a length that's long enough to tie comfortably around your waist. Center the Thread-and-Tape rectangle over the sheer fabric and sew together, on all four sides, to secure.

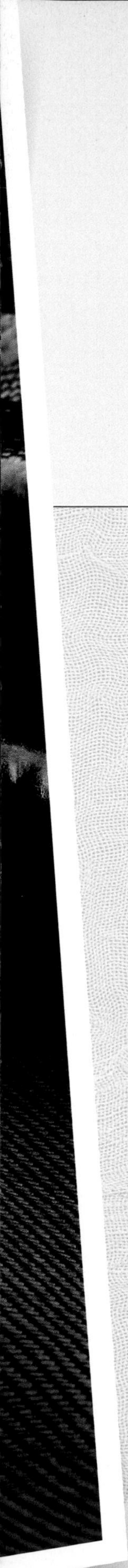

Eco-Stitch Brooch

Let the world know that you're a proud recycler with this recycled-

bag brooch. Of course, the bag puffs are so stylish, their origin might

not be obvious to the casual observer—a true example of how one

might make treasure from trash.

Featured Fabric: Bag Puff (see page 14).

Materials

muslin, scrap at least 4" × 2¾" (10cm × 7cm)

scissors

red plastic bag

large-eye needle

cardboard (heavy-weight)

fabric glue

epoxy

pin back

water-based dimensional adhesive/glaze
(optional)

1. Glue material to cardboard

Cut a piece of muslin to 4" × 2¾" (10cm × 7cm) and use the technique described on pages 14–15 to create Bag-Puff fabric with three puffs that are spaced ¼" (6mm) apart. Cut cardboard to 1" × 1¾" (3cm × 4cm). Center the bag-puff fabric on the cardboard. Use fabric glue to adhere the long sides of the fabric to the cardboard.

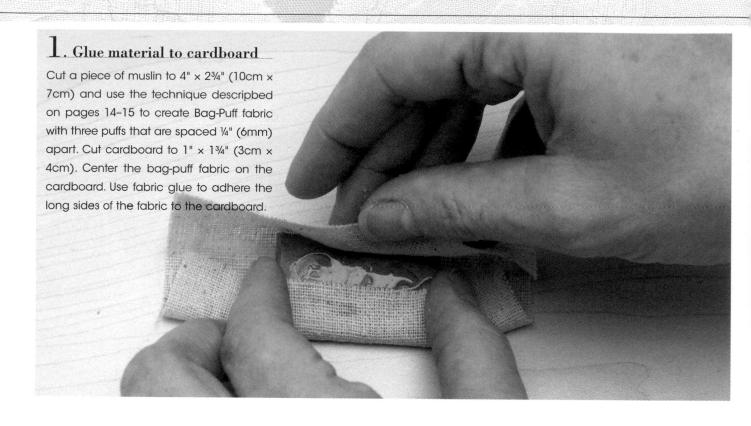

Loose Threads

Printed store bags work well for this fabric because the logos become part of the design.

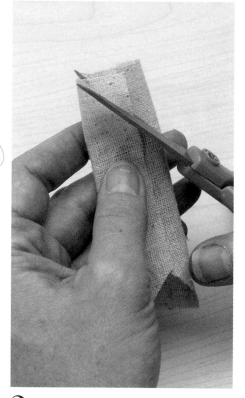

2. Cut and fold corners

Use scissors to notch a triangle from each of the corners of the fabric to eliminate bulk when folding.

3. Fold and adhere ends

Use more fabric glue to adhere the ends of the fabric to the back.

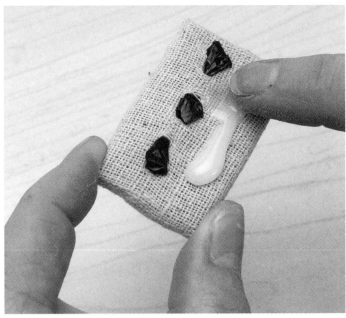

4. Add pin back

Use E-6000 adhesive to center the pin back to the back of the wrapped piece. (Please refer to manufacturer's safety instructions when using a strong adhesive.)

5. Apply dimentionsl adhesive/glaze (optional)

If you prefer a shiny texture, add a layer of water-based dimensional adhesive glaze to the top of the brooch.

Variations

Like the Eco-Stitch Brooch, this cuff starts off with rough muslin, a recycled bag and a needle. When cutting the fabric, measure the circumference of your wrist plus about 2" (5cm), and a bit extra to allow some fabric to fold over on all four sides, for a finished look. Create your puff stiches in the center portion only, and then fold and secure the edges under and add the closures. Wear this cuff to show off your playful outlook.

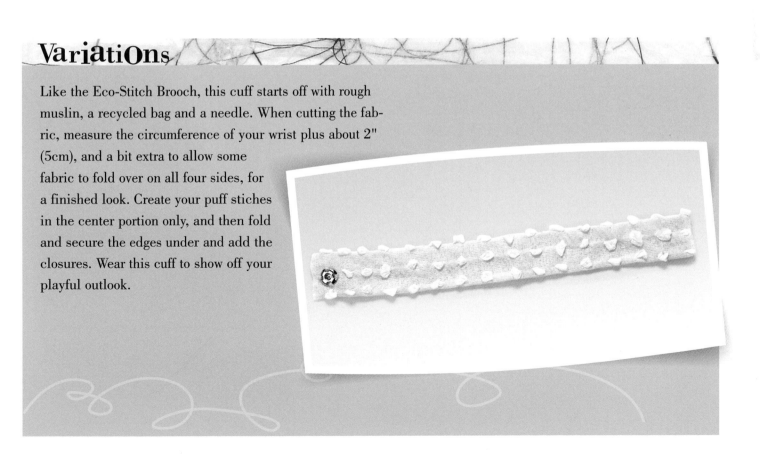

Red-Hot Night Clutch

This clutch is for a bold and daring evening out. Take it to dinner and the theater, but you'll be the one providing all of the drama with this bag's red lining and ornate details.

Featured Fabric: Loose Thread (see page 27).

Materials

taffeta in 2 colors, about a 12" (30cm) square of each

copy of clutch pattern (see page 120)

scissors

pins

sewing thread

sewing machine

handbag frame with screws

screwdriver (if needed for frame)

purse chain (optional)

1 Create loose threads

Cut a small notch at the edge of the taffeta fabric that will serve as the lining (here, red), and rip a strip. Pull the loose threads from the edge of the material. Roll the threads into a loose ball to keep together until you use them. Repeat with taffeta in the color chosen for the bag as well (here, black).

2 Cut pattern

Pin the pattern (see page 120) to the lining fabric and cut around it. Repeat to create an identical lining piece. Then repeat create two more pieces from the fabric that will be on the outside. Mark where the hinges of the purse frame stop on all of the pieces of the cut fabric.

3 Sew loose threads

Create a Loose-Thread fabric (page 27) by adding both sets of loose threads and sew onto one piece of the outer fabric. I created my design by sewing the loose threads of the lining taffeta first. Sew three to five lines to secure. Repeat the process for the second piece of the bag taffeta.

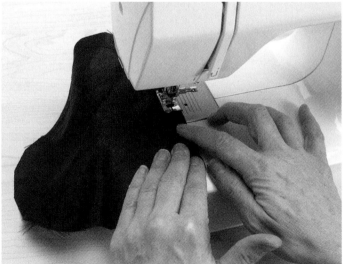

4 Sew purse seams

Position the outer taffeta pieces with Loose-Thread sides together. Starting at one of the marks for the hinge, straight stitch a standard seam allowance around to the second frame-hinge mark. Cut threads. Turn the top edge in ½" (1cm) and straight stitch it to secure.

5 Sew lining seams

Position the lining color taffeta pieces with right sides together. Starting at one of the marks for the hinge, straight stitch a standard seam allowance around to the second frame hinge mark. Cut the threads.

 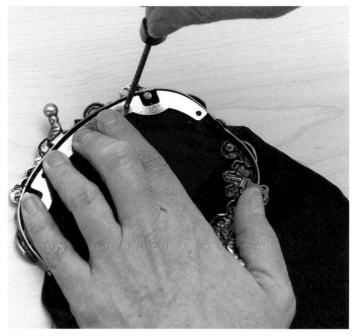

6 Sew lining to purse

Turn the bag right side out. Trim the seam allowance of the lining to eliminate bulk. Starting at the seam where the hinges meet, pin the lining to the purse. Repeat for other hinge seam. Then pin the top of the lining to the purse and stitch together. You don't have to change the thread color because this will all be hidden under the frame.

7 Attach purse frame

Attach frame according to manufacturer's instructions. (Shown: Line up the fabric seams with the hinges and press the fabric into the frame. Sandwich the purse and lining between the frame and the washer on one side. Attach the screws. Repeat for the other side.) Add chains.

Variations

This variation would work with a clutch of any size. Lay out the design for your Loop-to-Loop pattern (see page 23), and mark it accordingly. After you have completed the loops, attach the purse to the frame.

For this Give-and-Take clutch, you will need to sew and slash the outer fabric first. Following the creation of your fabric, you can cut the purse and lining out and then sew them together. Attach the frame, and out on the town you go.

Tree-on-the-Go Key Fob

The next time you're given a precious gift, save all of the enclosed tissue paper. Use it to make Paper-Fabric key fobs that you can give as gifts at your next party. Isn't recycling fun?

Featured Fabric: Paper Fabric (see page 16).

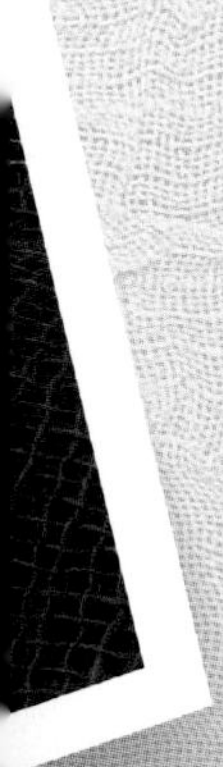

Materials

buckram or other stiff cotton, at least 3" × 8" (8cm × 20cm)

Paper Fabric swatch, at least 3" × 8" (8cm × 20cm)

large-eye needle

sewing thread in various colors and textures

sewing machine

scissors

keychain

water-based dimensional adhesive/glaze

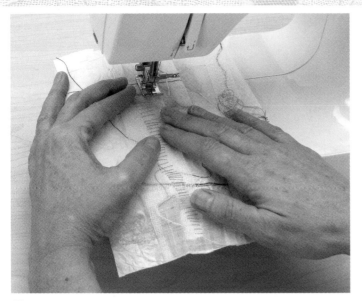

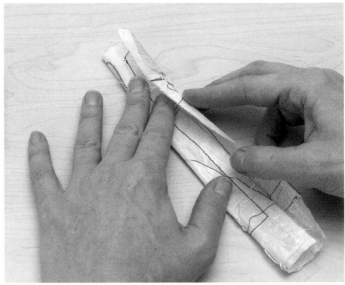

1 Embellish fabric

Embellish a swatch of Paper Fabric (see page 16) with hand-sewn stitches. Use a sewing machine to randomly straight stitch a piece of buckram to the fabric. Run a few more lines of stitches on the fabric to add stability.

2 Form fob shape

Cut the embellished Paper Fabric to 3" × 8" (8cm × 20cm). Fold the fabric in thirds, lengthwise.

Loose Threads

Sewing paper with the sewing machine is the same as sewing fabric. Make sure you have a sharp needle.

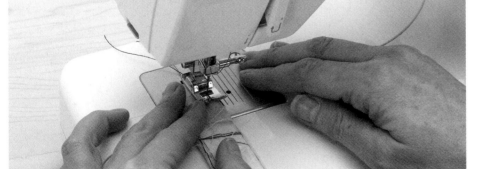

3 Sew edges

Straight stitch around all the edges to stabilize the material. Then, sew randomly to add texture.

Loose Threads

The most time consuming part of this project is drying the paper. Leave extra drying time for the top layer of glaze—it's worth the wait!

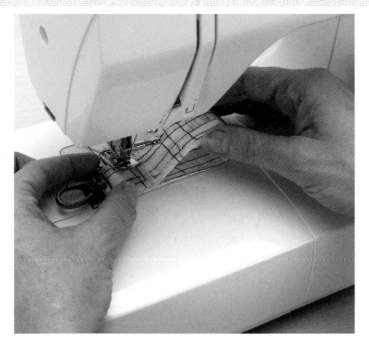

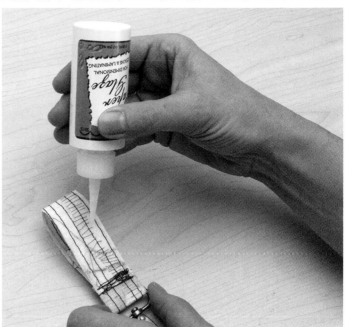

4 Attach clasp

Insert the sewn paper into a swivel clasp. Fold the end 1" (3cm) around the clasp. Fold the remaining fabric in half toward the clasp. Tuck this end under the 1" (3cm) end. Sew both pieces together on the 1" (3cm) flap.

5 Apply glaze

Apply a thick layer of water-based dimensional adhesive/glaze to the paper fabric. Spread evenly. Let dry.

Variations

After making the Paper Fabric, cut the paper to the size you want the clutch to be. Remember to add enough for a flap. I embellished my paper with some decorative hand stitches before it was put together. Now, stitch together the clutch on both sides with a sewing machine or by hand. Glue on the leather adornment, and a smashing clutch is all yours.

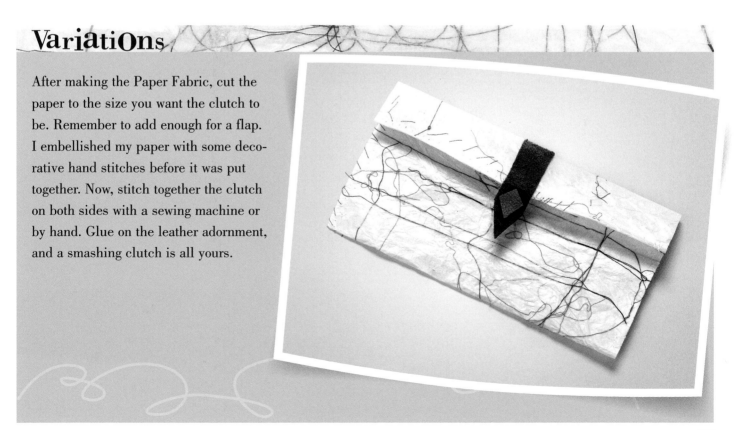

Trendy Green Belt

The scourge of the environment, the plastic bag, is the basis for this project. Instead of filling landfills, the plastic bag is made into thread and integrated into a fun wearable. I used a white bag with black printing, but just imagine all the different varieties of bags you can use and the effect the printing will create. As always, have fun wearing your one-of-a-kind stylish belt.

Featured Fabric: Bag Puff (see page 14).

Materials

nylon belting, about 2" x 44" (5cm x 112cm)

soft plastic bag

scissors

water-soluble dressmaker pencil

large-eye needle

2 2" (5cm) D rings

thread

sewing machine

1 Create bag puffs

Use nylon belting to create Bag-Puff material (see page 14). Use a water-soluble dressmaker pencil or chalk to mark material ½" (1cm) from edges and leave ½" (1cm) between puffs.

2 Attach D rings and finish

Slide both D rings onto the belting. Fold the material over ½" (1cm) to cover the D rings and straight stitch the material to secure it. Fold the other end of material over ½" (1cm) and sew a straight stitch to secure it in place.

CHAPTER 4

Outerwear

Here, you'll find projects for those days turning from cool to cold, but with these stunning items, your finished outfit will be hot! Edgy elegance surrounds the Haute Oddment Scarf (see page 102), while a loop-to-loop collar adds sophistication to the New York Fall Cape (see page 108). Whether you favor a scarflet or shawl, all of these projects will have others talking behind your back—in a good way!

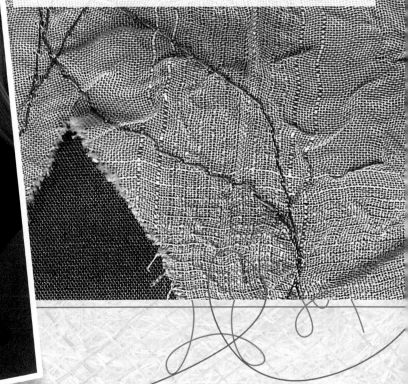

Haute Oddment Scarf

When you need something to jazz up an outfit, this scarf is the perfect solution. You can wear it as a belt or a scarf. The fake seam is simply a strip of fabric that you've sewn onto the scarf. Just finish the edges and snip the threads, and out the door you go.

Featured Fabric: Faux Seam (see page 30).

Materials

sheer fabric, about 52" × 17" (132cm × 43cm)

fabric for fake seams, 10 strips, about 17" × 1½" (132cm × 4cm)

scissors

sewing thread

sewing machine

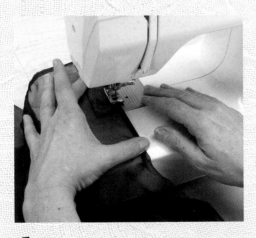

1 Finish all edges

Cut the sheer fabric to the size of the scarf desired (shown here as 52" × 17" [132cm × 43cm]). Create a ½" (1cm) straight-stitch hem on all edges by folding fabric in ¼" (6mm), two times.

2 Attach seam allowances

Begin adding fake seams by sewing ripped strips of fabric (the length of the sheer fabric) to the scarf, starting along an outside edge. Repeat for as many strips as desired, leaving about ½" (1cm) between strips.

Cozy Spring Scarflet

On days when it's too warm for a heavy sweater but not cool enough

for a long scarf, spruce up your outfit with this scarflet. The flower adds

a bit of romance without a lot of meticulous stitching, and the leaves

are actually cutout scraps, saved from previous Give-and-Take proj-

ects. You'll love the carefree methods used to get this unique look.

Featured Fabric: scraps from Give-and-Take (see page 32).

Materials

self-lined stretch ultra-suede, about 29" × 6" (74cm × 15cm)

scrap of satin, about 18" × 2" (46cm × 5cm)

leftover leaf-shaped cutouts from another project

water-soluble dressmaker pencil

sewing thread

sewing machine

precision-tip scissors

self-adhesive round Velcro fastener

1 Create hem

Cut the suede fabric to 29" x 6" (74cm x 15cm). Create a 1" (3cm) hem by folding in the edges ½" (1cm) twice and straight stitching along each.

2 Mark spot for flower

Use a water-soluble dressmaking pencil to mark where you want the center of the flower to be placed on the scarflet (here, 3" [8cm] from one side and 1½" [4cm] from the bottom edge).

Loose Threads

More than one fabric would work for this project. I used stretch ultra-suede because I love the silky softness of the underside against my skin.

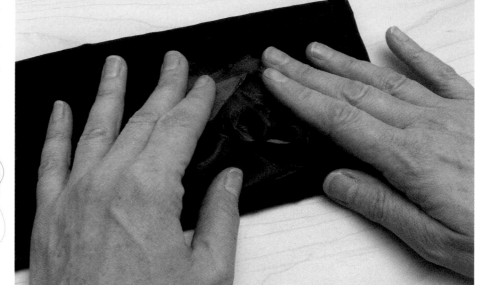

3 Create flower

With a piece of scrap satin that's 18" (46cm) in length, make a small cut approximately 1" (3cm) in from the edge. Rip the fabric to create a strip. Wrap the strip around itself to create petals.

A ½" (1cm) strip of fabric 4"–6" (10cm–15cm) long will make a small flower. Use 9" (23cm) or more of a 1" (3cm) strip for a larger flower.

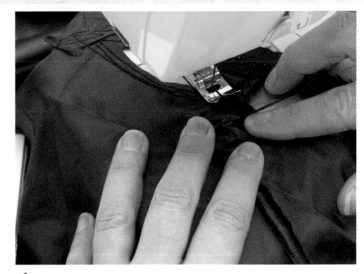

4 Add embellishments

Take a strip from the suede fabric and roll it into a spiral shape. Place the flower between the presser foot and the material, and randomly sew the flower onto the fabric. After the flower is loosely attached, use scissors to remove the tail of the strip of material. Sew a few more rows over the flower to secure.

5 Attach flower leaves

Take leftover leaf cutouts from a Give-And-Take project (see pages 32–33) and slide a few under the flower. Sew each one down its center to secure it to the fabric.

6 Attach fastener

Use a water-soluble dressmaker pencil to mark the center of the lining side of the fabric at the section where the flower is stitched down. Attach the fuzzy-loop half of a Velcro circle to the marked spot on the lining side, and apply the hook half of the Velcro circle to the front side of the other end of the scarf, where the two will overlap and meet up.

New York Fall Cape

Make a statement in this eyecatching cape. Its simple construction and

neutral fabric allow the loops to pop when created in a contrasting

color, or add subtle texture to a monochromatic palette.

Featured Fabric: Loop-to-Loop (see page 23).

Materials

fabric, medium to heavyweight, 66" x 56" (168cm x 142cm)

water-soluble dressmaker pencil

scissors

crochet thread

large-eye needle

large button or snap

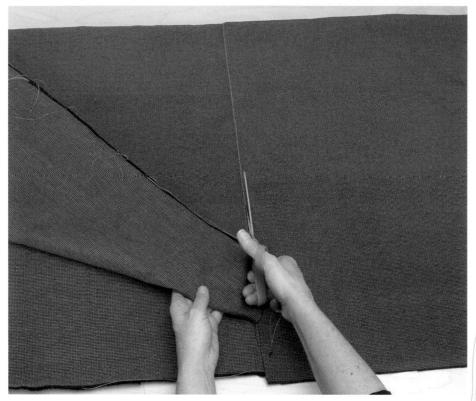

1 Create front opening

Fold the fabric in half to measure 66" × 28" (168cm × 71cm). Measure the center point of the fold and draw a vertical line from that point down the length of the fabric. Cut along the line on the top layer only. This will create the front opening of the cape.

Loose Threads

When choosing fabric for this cape, choose material that lays nicely on the body, is not too flimsy or too light, has some warmth to it but is not too heavy, and has a weave that's loose enough to create the Loop-to-Loop stitch without a problem.

2 Create neck

Insert the scissors on the center cut made in step 1 on the fold. Cut 5" (13cm) away from the center and along the fold to create the neck opening. Repeat in the opposite direction.

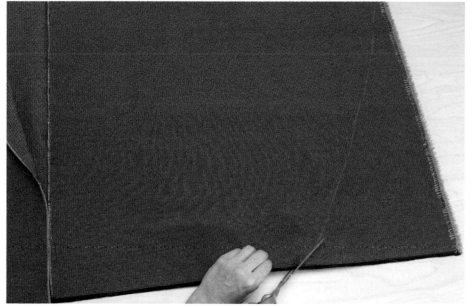

3 Curve outer edge

Along the bottom edge of the fabric, use a water-soluble dressmaker pencil or chalk to place a mark at 21½" (55cm) from the center cut made in step 1. On the side edge of the same half, place a mark at 2½" (6cm) below the fold. Draw a curved line to connect the two marks to form an arc. Cut both layers of material along the arc line to create a curved edge/corner. Repeat for the other side of the fabric, going in the opposite direction from the center cut. This should result in a completed shape for the cape that is almost elliptical.

4 Finish the neck

Turn the cape wrong side out. Starting at the center cut and working toward the shoulder, create a ½" (1cm) rolled edge by folding the neck edge in ¼" (6mm) twice. Pin if desired. Straight stitch the edge to hem it. Repeat the process for the top edge of the lapel. (Note: Don't sew the lapel to the cape. You're just finishing the top edge of the lapel.)

5 Finish bottom hem

With the cape still wrong side out, create a ½" (1cm) hem by folding the bottom edge in ¼" (6mm) twice. Pin if desired. Straight stitch the hem around the entire bottom edge of the cape.

Loose Threads

If your material frays when you cut it, save your threads for loose-thread projects!

6 Create Loop-to-Loop fabric

Use a water-soluble pencil or chalk to mark the lapels on the fabric. I marked my lapel so the side with the snap button top is 5" × 11" (13cm × 28cm) and the underside lapel with the male end of the snap is 5" × 13" (13cm × 33cm). Using crochet thread in the color of your choice, create Loop-to-Loop stitches (page 23) on the lapel.

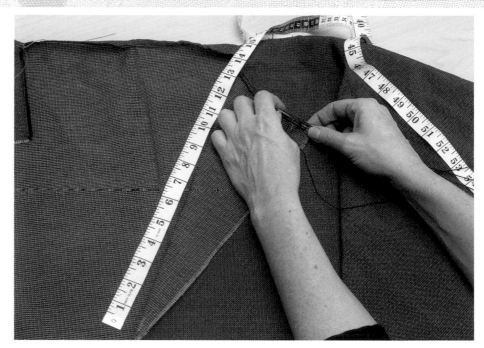

7 Finish cape

Use a needle and crochet thread to hand stitch the lapel down to the front of the cape. Add a snap or button under the lapel following the manufacturer's instructions. Fringe all the remaining edges of the cape (shown) or create a ½" (1cm) hem by rolling the edge under ¼" (6mm) twice and straight stitching.

Variations

This sophisticated stitch adds detail and a wonderful decorative element to a simple tank, gloves and cap. You can vary the length of your stitches and create really shaggy loops. Again, look for open-weave fabrics. Knit items are perfect for this.

When you're creating the loops, stretch the fabric and pull the loops so they're large enough to see. If you omit this step, the loops will be too tight and will look like a straight line, instead of a series of loops.

Loose Threads

If the fabric you choose doesn't have lines to follow, use a water-soluble dressmaking pencil to mark the lines for the loops.

Green-Couture Shawl

Perfect for your next fundraiser, the satin fabric of this shawl creates elegance and sophistication. If you decide to focus on the cutouts and not use the leftover leaves, be sure to save them for a later project. You never know when a leaf embellishment might provide just the right touch. This piece is contructed from one long, single rectangle of fabric, so it's quick and easy.

Featured Fabric: Give-and-Take (see page 32).

Materials

brown satin 94" × 21" (239cm × 53cm)

rotary cutter

cutting mat

sewing thread, 2 colors

1 Create Give-and-Take fabric

Working in small sections at a time, fold the fabric multiple times (accordion-style if you prefer) so that the folds are parallel with the short end of the fabric. Leaving about 2" (5cm) of space at each edge for finishing, cut out leaf shapes. Continue down the length of the fabric until both long sides are complete.

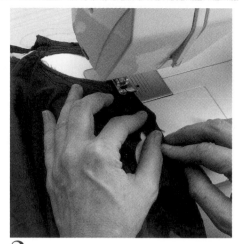

2 Stabilize cutouts

Use your sewing machine and straight stitch around the cutouts. Don't worry about straight lines or precision. These stitches stabilize the cutouts and add a decorative element. Repeat two or three times using the same or different color of thread. Create a hem around the entire piece by folding the fabric ¼" (6mm) twice and then using a straight stitch.

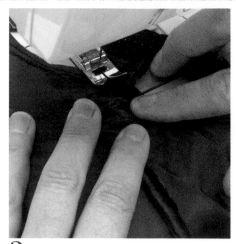

3 Add embellishments

Use a straight stitch to attach the leaf cutouts from step 1 in areas between and around the negative spaces. Add flower embellishments too (see pages 106–107), if you'd like.

Loose Threads

When you're attaching the cutouts, add some fun and visual interest by having the edges overlap the edges of the hem on the main fabric.

Variations

The Green Couture Shawl was created from a wonderful chocolate satin, which gives it an air of sophistication on the town. With that same Give-and-Take technique, you can make a smashing belt. I chose two contrasting fabrics and cut the oval shapes from the blue fabric first. I then sewed the two fabrics together to create the belt and added the cutouts as decorative elements.

Templates

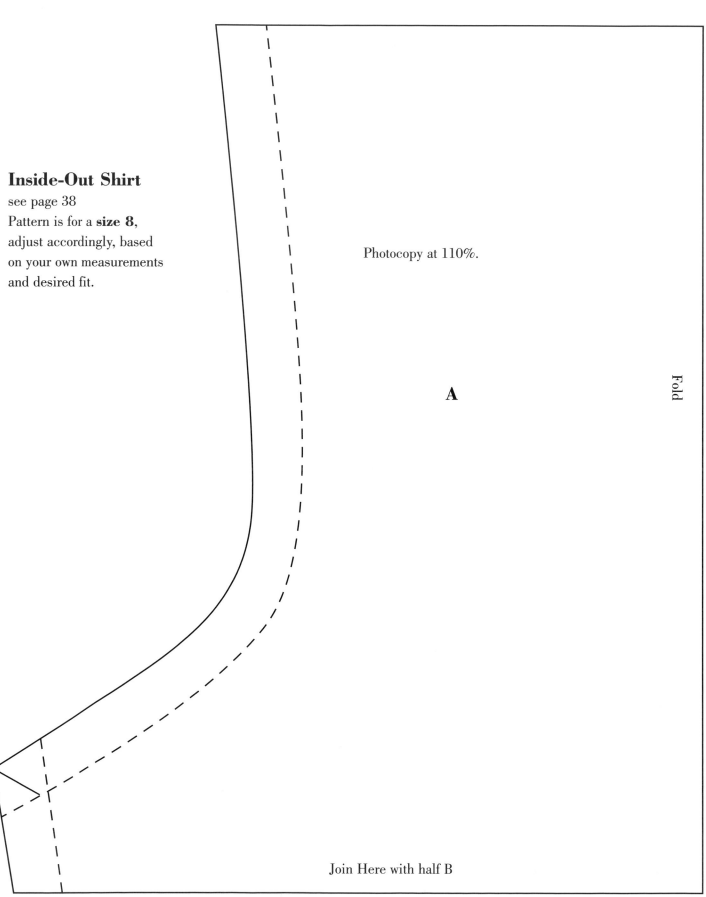

Inside-Out Shirt

see page 38
Pattern is for a **size 8**,
adjust accordingly, based
on your own measurements
and desired fit.

Photocopy at 110%.

A

Fold

Join Here with half B

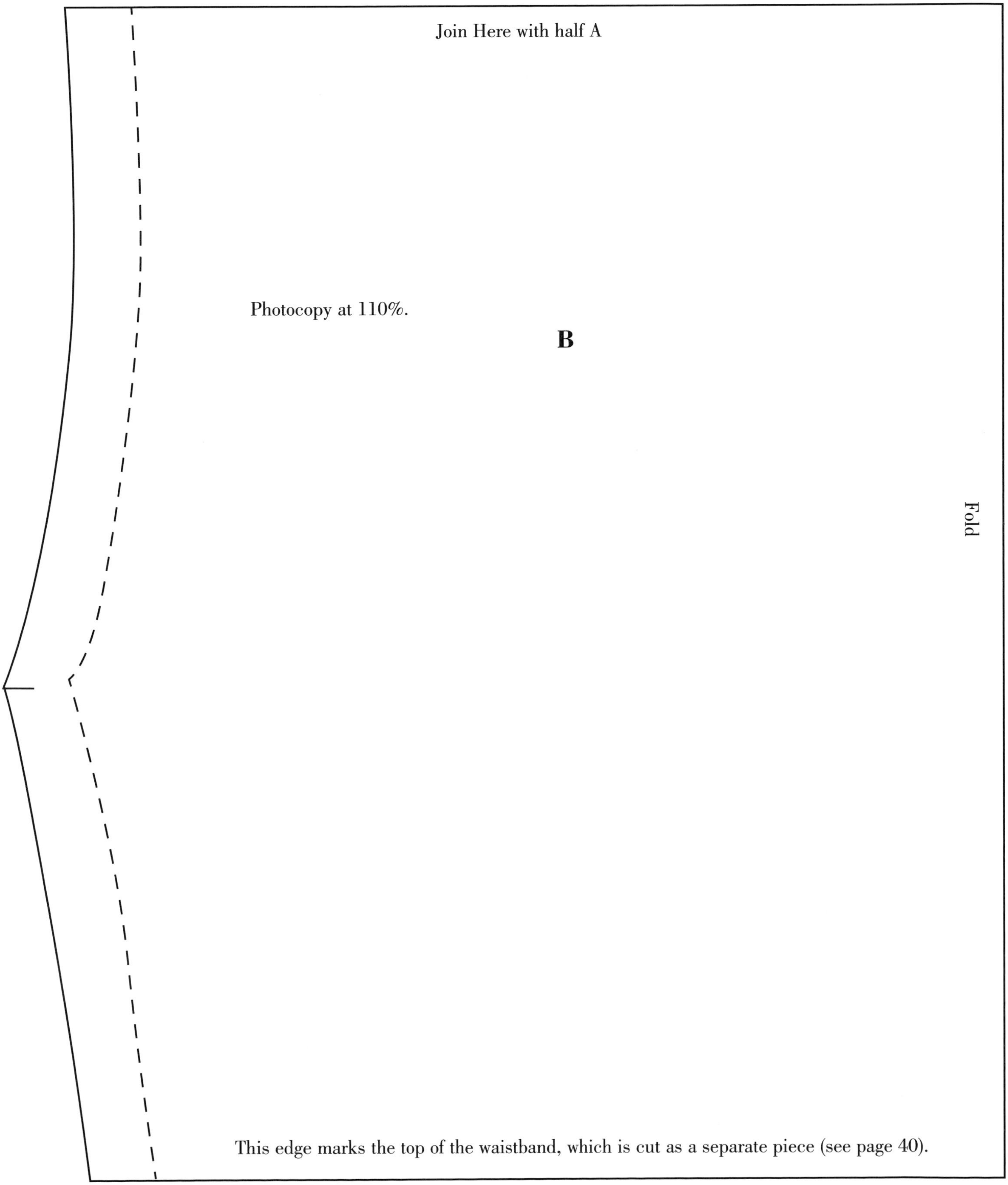

Join Here with half A

Photocopy at 110%.

B

Fold

This edge marks the top of the waistband, which is cut as a separate piece (see page 40).

Templates

Red-Hot Night Clutch
See page 90

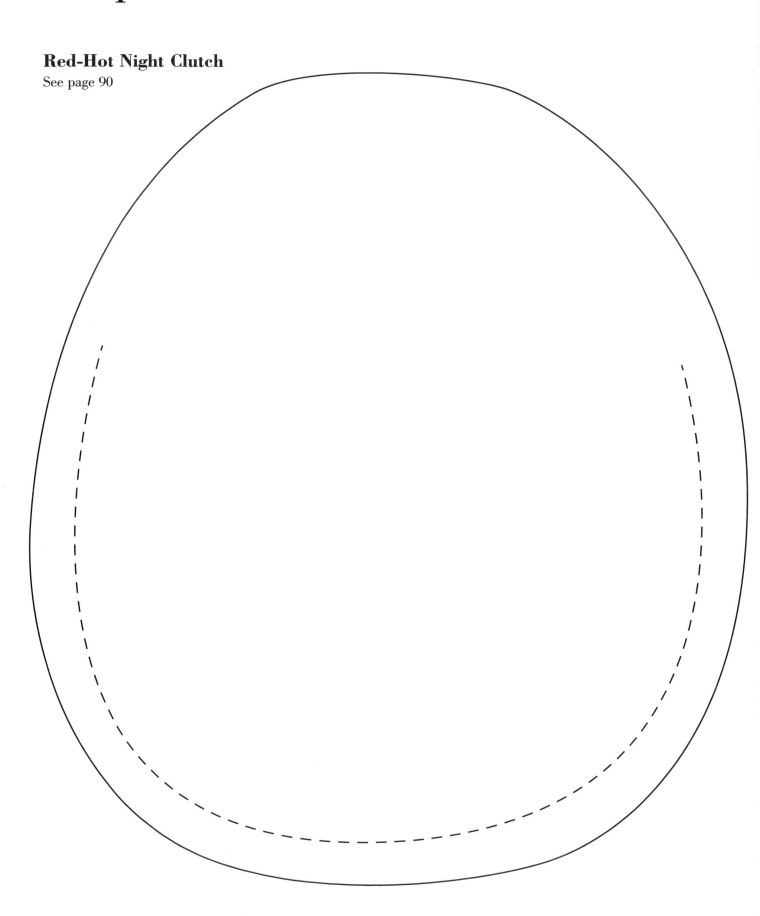

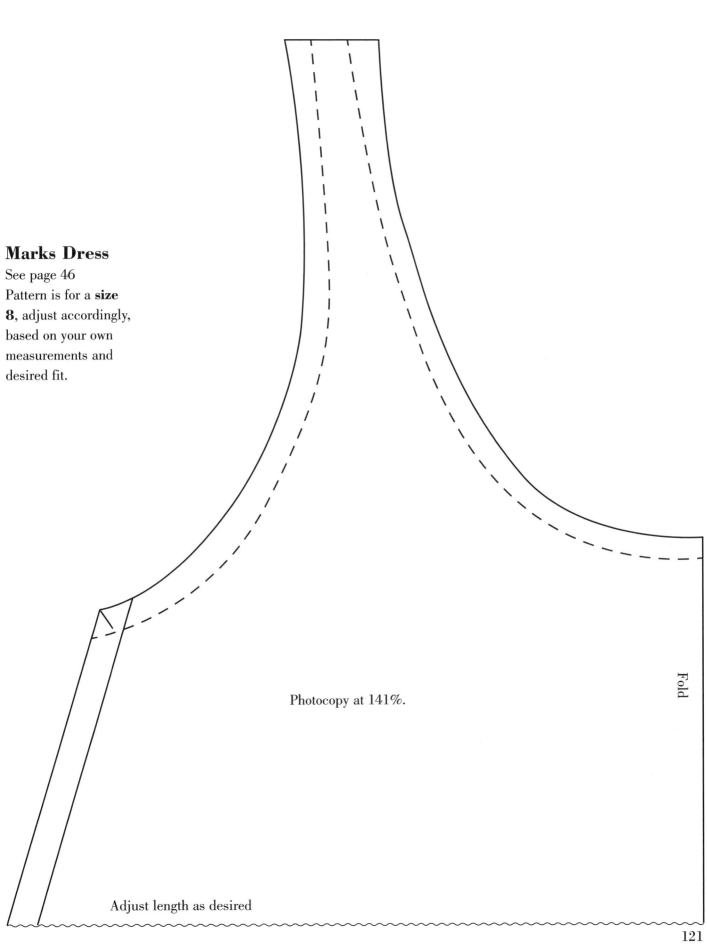

Marks Dress
See page 46
Pattern is for a **size 8**, adjust accordingly, based on your own measurements and desired fit.

Photocopy at 141%.

Fold

Adjust length as desired

121

Resources

Sewing Machines

Bernina
www.bernina.com

Brother
www.brother-usa.com/homesewing

Husqvarna Viking
www.husqvarnaviking.com

Janome
www.janome.com

Pfaff
www.pfaff.com

Singer
www.singerco.com

Fabric

Fabric Depot
www.fabricdepot.com

Fashion Fabrics Club
www.fashionfabricsclub.com

Reprodepot Fabrics
www.reprodepot.com

Vogue Fabrics
www.voguefabricsstore.com

Thread

Mary Maxim

www.marymaxim.com

Royal Yarns International

www.royalyarns.com

Sewing Tools

Fiskars

www.fiskars.com

Prym Consumer USA Inc.

www.dritz.com

Jewelry-Making Supplies

Fire Mountain Gems

www.firemountaingems.com

Rings & Things

www.rings-things.com

UMX Fashion Supplies

www.umei.com

Places I Find Inspiration

Artists, Blogs & General Websites

www.annwood.net/blog

www.artpropensity.com

www.assemblage.typepad.com

www.black-dog-knits.blogspot.com

www.bobilina.blogspot.com

www.creaturecomforts.typepad.com

www.decor8blog.com

www.dogwoodstudio.blogspot.com

www.elmorisette.blogspot.com

www.elsita.typepad.com

www.thefabricofmeditation.blogspot.com

www.guerzonmills.com

www.hellejorgensen.typepad.com

www.isabelhenao.com.co

www.jenworden.com

www.karenleslie.com

www.amyhuddleston.com

www.fakenature.com

www.herzensart.com

www.maryannwakeley.com

www.marybogdan.com

www.outsapop.com

www.questaoquella.blogspot.com

www.ruthsinger.com

www.sixandahalfstitches.typepad.com

www.stacyalexander.blogspot.com

www.theresahalldesigns.com

Education

www.fineartclasses.com

Etsy Shops

www.cccoeteam.etsy.com (click favorites)

www.greenmandesigns.etsy.com

www.kjoo.etsy.com

www.lorimarsha.etsy.com

Magazines

www.americancraftmag.org

www.bellearmoir.com

www.craftzine.com

www.fiberartsmagazine.com

www.bellearmoire.com

www.ornamentmagazine.com

www.selvedge.org

www.makezine.com

www.marthastewart.com

Index

Indulge Yo... ...de with These
Other Great North Light Books

Canvas ...
Alisa B...

Learn ...
look of ...
and on...
everyth...
ings to...
Inside...
find m...
for con...
and canvas in totally unexpected w...
inspired art may not give you insta...
you've mastered these techniques,...
sure to earn you a reputation.

ISBN-13: 978-1-60061-075-2
ISBN-10: 1-60061-075-7
paperback • 128 pages
Z1844

Plush You!
Kristen Rask

This showcase of 100 plush
toys, many with patterns and
instructions, will inspire you
to join in on the DIY toy phe-
nomenon. The wildly popular
Plush You! show is now avail-
...with pictures of each contribution,
...ning features such as plushie bios. The
...this book provide instant gratification
...new ideas for experienced toymakers.
...tures and lovable monsters, along with
...of beef and other squeezable subjects,
...stible book that you just want to hug.

...6-4
...0961
paperback with flaps • 144 pages
Z0951

AlterNation
*Shannon Okey and
Alexandra Underhill*

Hey, you, indie-crafter—
yeah, you, crafty chick
with the scissors. Check
out *AlterNation*, the DIY
fashion bible that shows
you how to personalize your
wardrobe with a wide range
of no-sew and low-sew techniques. This book has lots of
cool stuff to make, like tie skirts, scrap scarves, plus oh
so much more. Just follow the step-by-step instructions,
and you'll soon be a total pro at making your own clothing
and accessories.

ISBN-10: 1-58180-978-6
ISBN-13: 978-1-58180-978-7
paperback • 144 pages
Z0713

Warm Fuzzies
Betz White

Warm Fuzzies is filled with
techniques, tips and patterns
for creating 30 cute and colorful felted projects, including cozy pillows and throws
as well as comfortable hats,
scarves, pincushions and
handbags. Author Betz White
will show you how to felt thrift store and bargain sweaters,
then cut them up and use them to make quick, adorable
projects for the whole family. Learn how to select the best
knitted wool for felting, the best way to full it, and how
to combine this process with a wide variety of other techniques, including appliqué, knitted I-cord, basic embroi-
dery, needle felting, pre-felting manipulation and more.

ISBN-10: 1-60061-007-2
ISBN-13: 978-1-60061-007-3
paperback • 144 pages
Z1026

These books and other fine North Light titles are available at your local craft retailer,
bookstore or online supplier, or visit us at www.mycraftivity.com.